D1211770

Singular architect

Josep Liz, Pere Vivas, Ricard Pla

TRIANGLE▼BOOKS

Casa Vicens
El Capricho
Pavellons Güell
Palau Güell
Col·legi de les Teresianes
Palacio Episcopal de Astorga
Casa Botines
Cellers Güell
Casa Calvet
Torre Bellesguard
Park Güell
Catedral de Mallorca
Casa Batlló
La Pedrera
Cripta de la Colònia Güell
Basílica de la Sagrada Família

10 exclusive videos:

Look at Antoni Gaudí's works on your smartphone or tablet.

GAUDÍ
Singular architect

Casa Batlló

GAUDÍ Singular architect

Despite the vast amount written in recent decades about the architecture of Antoni Gaudí (Reus, 1852–Barcelona, 1926) and despite the relative closeness in time of his work, the perception that the non-specialised public has of the architect and his creations is surrounded by a halo of legend, which, while increasing the admiration for his figure and his work in all the corners of the world, at the same time does not provide a clear positioning in the scheme of western art history beyond a general and ambiguous "modernism".

Gaudí was a contemporary of Van Gogh, Matisse, Gauguin and Cézanne, postimpressionists and initiators of modern art, and Henri H. Richardson, William Le Baron Jenney and Louis H. Sullivan, creators of the Chicago School with the first modern skyscrapers; he produced his principal works (La Pedrera, Park Güell, the church of the Colonia Güell or the schools of the Sagrada Família) at the same time that Picasso and Braque introduced cubism and some years before the emblematic expressionist buildings of Rudolf Steiner (the second Goetheanum) or Erich Mendelsohn (the Einstein Tower); he introduced the modular construction with prefabricated elements 20 years before Lloyd Wright in Hollyhock House or Casa Barnsdall (1922), and he applied the criteria of integrating environmental factors of the site (use, function, native materials or constructive processes) in the creation of his buildings half a century before Scandinavian architects or Lloyd Wright himself formalised the movement of "organic architecture".

Where, then, can we place Gaudí? George R. Collins (1960) states that although Gaudí has his explanation in the historical context of the Catalonia of the second half of the 19th century, as an artist he is a unique case, without forerunners, like all geniuses, and without almost any disciples or followers beyond his collaborators and often friends of the grand master (Francesc Berenguer, Josep Maria Jujol, Joan Rubió Bellver, Domènec Sugrañes, Lluís Bonet, Isidre Puig Boada, Joan Bergós, Francesc Folguera, Cèsar Martinell, Josep F. Ràfols) who shared his work in

The Sunflowers, Vincent van Gogh, 1888.

El Capricho, Antoni Gaudí, 1883-1885.

Water lilies, Claude Monet, 1895-1926.

Casa Batlló, Antoni Gaudí, 1898-1900.

a small circle of admirers, and who after Gaudí's death hardly left a mark or outstanding works.

Perhaps this is due to the emphatically reserved character of Gaudí or to his often intuitive constructive methods —almost never working according to his original plans and he found new solutions and designs as the work progressed— but the fact is he never thought it relevant to inform in writing or at international congresses, etc. of an explicit architectural theory, unlike the majority of contemporary or immediately following architects who would be represented in the history of modern architecture not only for their buildings, but also an intensive theoretical activity and the diffusion of their philosophy. One example clearly demonstrates this: in 1910 Gaudí turned down an invitation from Güell to accompany him to Paris to explain the project of the Sagrada Família and he sent in his place Jeroni Martorell with these instructions: "In Paris they will not understand this architecture and it will cause controversy; if they ask you what it is, tell them: a perfecting of Gothic. They will go mad and say things. Only when they don't have anything left to say, confirm again that it is a perfecting of Gothic, and nothing else".

Perhaps the conjuncture of the first third of the 20th century was not his time: he showed an extreme tension between what was "new" (a demand of youth, break with the past, re-conquest of a new simplicity) and what was "old" (acceptance of multiplicity, complexity, in brief, of old age), a concept to which Gaudí was associated by his contemporary compatriots due not only to his exuberant "decorations" and external forms, but also certainly for his emphatic religiousness —in a Catalonia in which the progressive forces were deeply anti-clerical— and the close relationships he had with his sponsors: religious orders, bishops and aristocrats, especially Count Güell, champion of the Spanish monarchy. Gaudí considered the work of an architect an instrument of divinity and the forms he used, even the structural ones, had an iconographic meaning: the hyperbolic paraboloid, for example (generated by a

Casa Botines,
Antoni Gaudí, 1892.

Cincinnati Chamber of Commerce,
Henry, H. Richardson, 1889.

Old Chicago Stock Exchange,
Louis Sullivan, 1893-1894.

straight line that moves over another two on a different plane), he identified as a symbol of the Holy Trinity. In fact, Gaudí's religious feelings had put his own life in danger when he undertook such an extreme fast that bishop Torres i Bages himself had to intervene to convince him to end it. This same feeling led him to abandon, when he was at the peak of his career, all the secular projects to devote himself entirely to what he considered his life project: the temple of the Sagrada Família.

Or, finally, perhaps it is due to the situation of absolute cultural, economic and political periphery regarding Europe and the United States into which Spain had fallen after two centuries of decadence following its period of hegemony during the 16th and 17th centuries.

Whatever the reason, in the first decades of the 20th century, his work remained in a discrete oblivion —the majority of foreign architects and theoreticians did not pay the least attention to him despite the occasional positive comment by Le Corbusier (1928) or Walter Gropius (1932), both in the Barcelona press— if not in scornful incomprehension, the case of his Catalan contemporaries who often satirised his creations, calling them ridiculous and of poor taste.

Although even in 1933 Salvador Dalí, a compatriot of Gaudí, demanded a reappraisal of him in his article "De la beauté terrifiante et comestible de l'architecture Modern Style" and brought him to the attention of the *avant garde*, especially the surrealist movement, the name of Gaudí does not appear in the essays of Henry-Russell Hitchcock (1929), Nikolau Pevsner (1936) or Sigfried Giedion (1941). It was not until the mid-20th century the importance of the Gaudian specialism and original contribution to the world of architecture and art in general began to be appreciated. First it was Bruno Zevi (1945, 1948 and 1949) on relating him with organicist authors such as Wright and Aalto; and a few years later appeared the first monographic works and studies: Cèsar Martinell (publication in several languages in 1955), H. R. Hitchcock (exhibition in New York

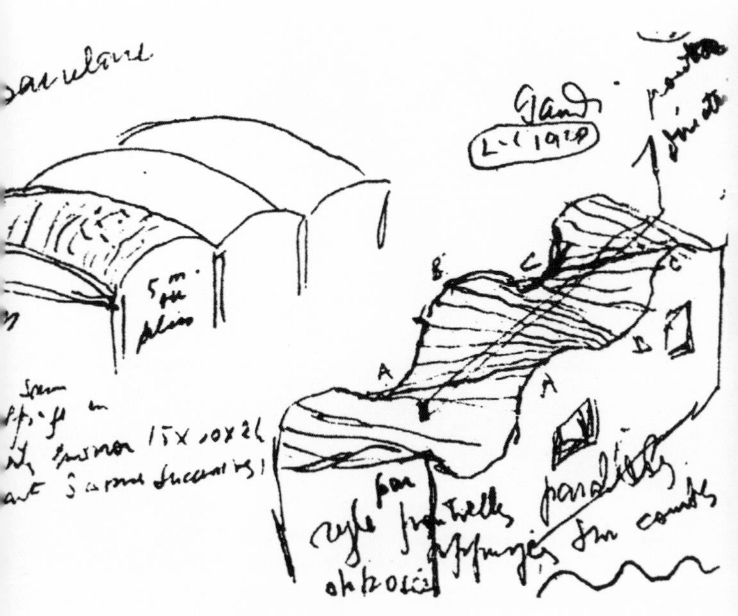

Drawing of the Sagrada Família schools made by Le Corbusier in 1928.

Sagrada Família Schools, Antoni Gaudí, 1909.

and publication in English in 1956 and 1957) and, above all —the works of Martinell and Hitchcok were very brief— George R. Collins, who in 1960 published, in English, the first monograph about Gaudí.

The world could ignore Gaudí but Gaudí was up to date with what was going on. He knew of the work of John Ruskin —with whom he coincided ideologically on the importance of the spiritual side of art—; he knew the works of the symbolists, the pre-Raphaelites, William Morris and the Arts and Crafts movement, Viollet-le-Duc and his theories of restoration —all of them referents of Catalan Modernism—, and also of the French impressionists (façade of Casa Batlló) or the Chicago School (curtain wall of La Pedrera); and was well aware of the proposals of Le Corbusier, for example, of whom he stated "was a builder of boxes". Gaudí, however, carried out his work with independence and originality and transcended the narrow frameworks of styles. In the words of Daniel Giralt-Miracle, general curator of the Gaudí International Year (2002), the architect was "a powerful and excessive artist, capable of breaking with the loyalty to historical styles and of rethinking the very essence of architecture reconsidering materials, procedures, techniques, systems of calculus or geometric repertoires".

Gaudí —despite the first thing to attract one's attention to his work being the use of an exhilarating polychrome or very expressive naturalist forms, almost gifted with movement— is a creator ruled by the logic of rationality and functionalism and was the first architect who used the principles of ruled geometry of warped surfaces (which enabled him to imitate the forms of nature) applied to the construction of buildings, as well as that already mentioned regarding modular construction or the application of integrating environmental factors. He worked forming multidisciplinary teams with which he shared the responsibility of the work and encouraged them to intervene decisively (as in the case of Jujol on the bench of Park Güell or the ceilings of La Pedrera, to give just one

Goetheanum,
Rudolf Steiner, 1924-1928.

Einstein Tower,
Erich Mendelsohn, 1917-1924.

La Pedrera,
Antoni Gaudí, 1906-1912.

Dominus

example). Also, in many spheres of contemporary art, he progressed along paths that others found some time later. This is the case of the collages of Park Güell and of compositions of *trencadís* close to the work of the post-surrealist Miró or American abstract expressionism, and even, as in the ceilings of La Pedrera, before Apollinaire coined the term calligram and declared to his friend Picasso "anch'io son' pittore!" (I am also a painter!), Gaudí left three-dimensional examples of graphic poetry.

Collins, in the abovementioned monograph wrote: "The strength of Antoni Gaudí as an architect lies in his prolific invention of forms. The variety of expression of these forms in themselves, as sculptures or paintings, would feature him as a notable modern artist. However, in fact, they are the result of some extraordinary structural inventions, of an imaginative use of materials and of an unequalled sense of decoration..., three traditional attributes of a master architect. If we add to this ability the intangible factors of the architecture, such as the space, colour and light, we will understand why the architectural world of our times focuses its attention on his relatively few works".

Gaudí is an extraordinary and unrepeatable architect, with great coherence between his exuberant façades and roofs, his humanised habitable spaces and his constructive systems. His speciality, according to the expert Joan Bassegoda, is the architecture of natural reality although presented as if it were the result of an illusion, almost a fairy tale.

Today almost no-one doubts the value of the contribution of the figure of Antoni Gaudí to the history of art in general and architecture in particular and architects such as Jean Nouvel or Frank Gehry, among others, consider him a precursor; his work is world-renowned by the general public and by architects and art historians as brilliant creation, in other words, that it "generates" (the work of an authentic creator), and UNESCO bears witness to this on awarding quite a few of his buildings the category of World Heritage Site.

Paintings above the choir stalls of the Cathedral of Mallorca, Gaudí, 1904-1914.

Collage on the ceiling soffits of the hypostyle hall of Park Güell, Gaudí, 1900-1914.

"Llum ne raija" (The light flows), one of the inscriptions or graphic poems on the ceilings of La Pedrera, Gaudí, 1906-1912.

GAUDÍ Comparative chronology

1838

Queen Victoria
United Kingdom

1844

Joan Güell opens the mechanised textile Vapor Vell factory
Sants (Barcelona)

1847

Marx and Engels begin to write the **Communist Manifesto,** published in 1848

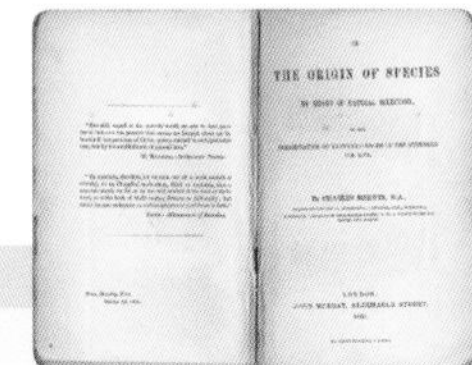

1859

Darwin
The Origin of the Species

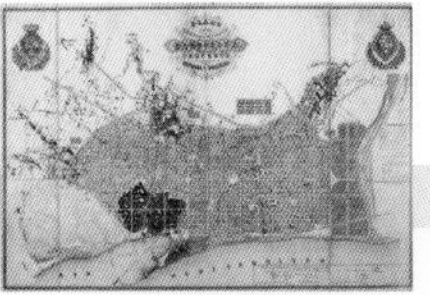

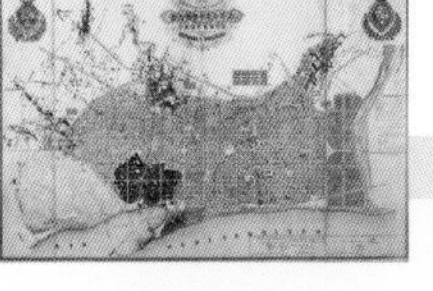

1860

Ildefons Cerdà
designs the Eixample district of Barcelona

1865

Abolition of slavery in the USA

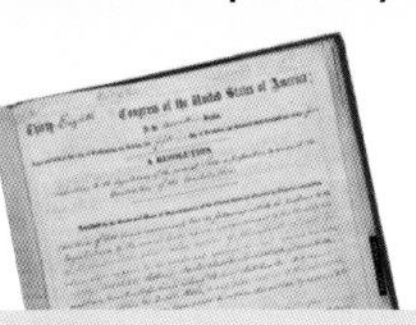

1867

Karl Marx
Capital

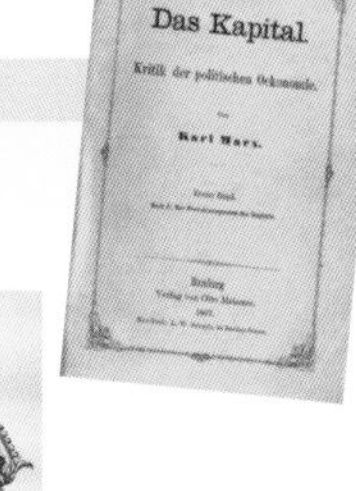

1875

Helena Blavatsky
Isis Unveiled

Creation of the Theosophical Society

Realm of Alfonso XII
1875-1885

1877

Jacint Verdaguer
L'Atlàntida

1879

Edison invents the electric lightbulb

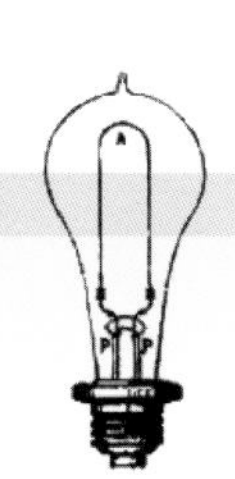

1881

Coronation of the Virgin of Montserrat

1884

Güell pavilions
1884-1887

1886

Palau Güell
1886-1888

1887

Car invented

1888

Theresan College
1888-1890

Universal Exhibition of Barcelona

1893

Eduard Munch
The Scream

Bomb in the Liceu

1894

Marconi invents the radio

1895

Güell Bodegas
1895-1901

The Lumière brothers invent the cinematograph

1897

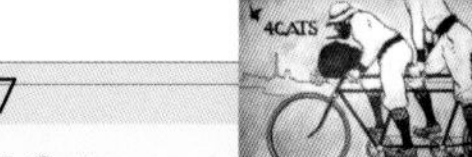

Els 4 Gats
a meeting point for the Barcelona avant-garde

1903

Cathedral of Mallorca
1903-1914

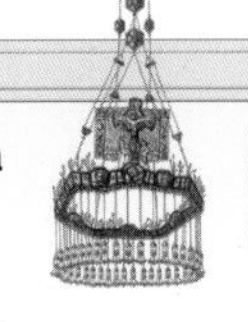

Marie Curie
Nobel Prize for Physics

Primer piloted flight

1904

Casa Batlló
1904-1907

1905

Albert Einstein
Theory of Relativity

Palau de la Música Catalana

Claude Debussy
The Sea

1906

La Pedrera
1906-1912

Ramón y Cajal
Nobel Prize for Medicine

1916

DADA Manifesto

1917

Russian Revolution

1918

End of the First World War
1914-1918

1919

Bauhaus

1848

First photograph in Barcelona
Pla de Palau

1852

Antoni Gaudí i Cornet
Reus was born

1853

Otis invents the lift

1858

Narcís Monturiol invents the first crewed submarine and tests it in Barcelona in 1859

1868

La Gloriosa, revolution in Spain that signifies the dethroning of Queen **Isabel II**

1870

Jules Verne
Twenty-thousand leagues under the Sea

1871

Paris Commune

1873

I Spanish Republic
1873-1874

1883

Chicago School

The Nau Gaudí
1883

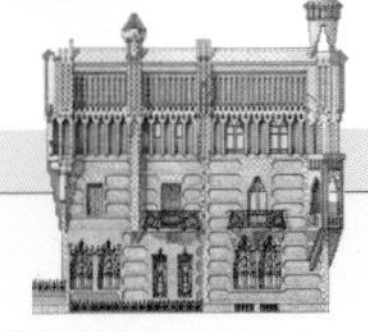

Casa Vicens
1883-1888

El Capricho
1883-1885

Sagrada Família
1883-1926

1889

Episcopal Palace of Astorga
1889-1893

Eiffel Tower

Buffalo Bill in Barcelona

1890

Jazz
1890-1910

1892

Casa Botines
León

1898

Casa Calvet
1898-1900

Independence of Cuba

1899

First trolley bus in Barcelona

1900

Bellesguard Tower
1900-1909

Park Güell
1900-1914

First flight of the Zeppelin

Sigmund Freud
The interpretation of dreams

1907

Pablo Picasso
Les Demoiselles d'Avignon

Gustav Klimt
The Kiss

1908

Crypt of the Colònia Güell
1908-1915

1909

Tragic Week in Barcelona

1913

The Liceu premieres Wagner's *Parsifal*

1925

Sagrada Família
Pinnacle of Saint Barnabus

1926

Gaudí dies
Barcelona

Television invented

1929

International Exhibition of Barcelona

La Nau Gaudí
Casa Vicens
El Capricho
Pavellons Güell
Palau Güell
Col·legi de les Teresianes
Palacio Episcopal de Astorga
Casa Botines

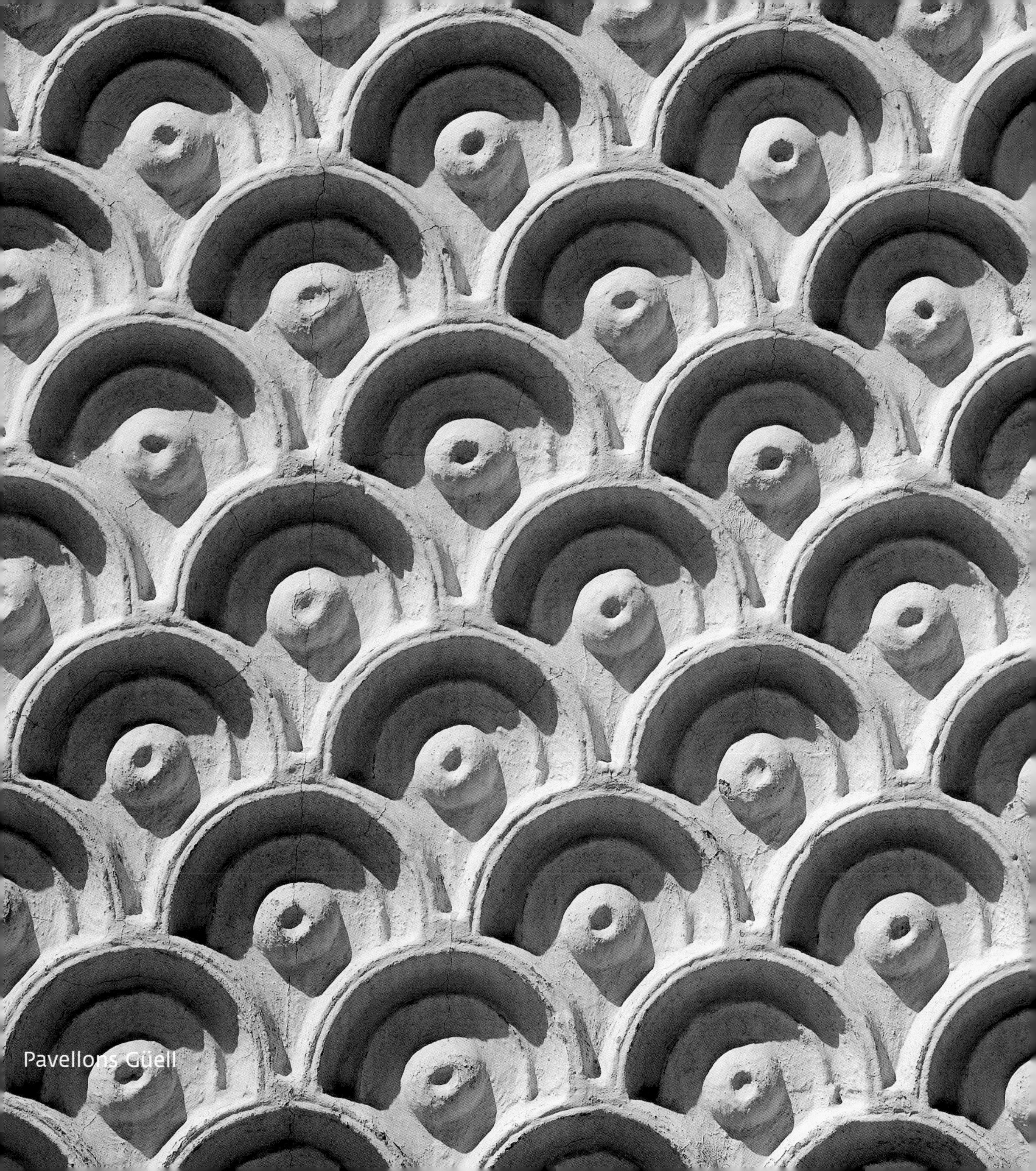
Pavellons Güell

La Nau Gaudí

Mataró Carrer Cooperativa, 47

La Nau Gaudí

1883

An industrial warehouse used to bleach cotton fabric built by La Obrera Mataronense, a cooperative textile company founded in 1864. This single-storey industrial building has the singularity of being the first that Gaudí built and in which he already applied architectural solutions such as parabolic arches.

Indeed, in the Nau Gaudí –the popular name by which this construction is known– the young architect already shows the relevance that constructive studies and systems had for him and covers almost 600 square metres without using columns or walls, but articulating small sections of wood with bolts to form the 12 slender and resistant arches of 12 m span that create a diaphanous interior space. Over these arches, some beams support a gabled roof and enable the construction of side walls with large windows to let in the natural light.

The Nau Gaudí formed part of a much more ambitious complex that included thirty single-family housing units for the workers, a social centre, a school and a small construction that housed the toilets. Gaudí only managed to build one or two houses (today disappeared) and the small toilet building. Also, before the company went bankrupt at the end of the 1880s, he designed the standard of the cooperative, on which appears a loom with two bees (symbol of industry) and one can appreciate the calligraphy of the period when Gaudí was a student.

The Nau Gaudí was declared a Historical-Artistic Monument by the Spanish State in 1969 and a Cultural Asset of National Interest by the Generalitat de Catalunya (Autonomous Government) in 1982, and can legitimately be considered the starting point of Gaudian work. Today it is owned by Mataró Council and, after a respectful restoration by the architect Manuel Brullet, it houses the Bassat Collection of Contemporary Art.

Small toilet building. The ornamental tops of doors, windows and roof already show the Gaudian aesthetic of the following works.

Drawing by Gaudí for the standard of the Cooperative.

Detail of the rear façade of the Casino according to the design by Gaudí.

Parabolic arches of the Nau Gaudí.

Casa Vicens

Barcelona Carrer de les Carolines, 18

Casa Vicens

1883-1888

A bucolic retreat

Casa Vicens was situated on the corner of the estate and had a splendid garden in which the plants and the reflections of the water from the waterfall and fountain created a bucolic atmosphere, giving an early indication of the treatment that nature would be given during the modernist period.

Photographs from the time show a terrace that opens out to the garden with wooden, oriental-style blinds. This detail, along with the Arab smoking room on the ground floor, shows the oriental tendency, one of the fads of the time which, combined with the picturesque naturalism, formed a space that reflected another tendency of the period: escapism. The final aim is the search for a corner of beauty isolated from the grey world that was being created during industrialisation.

The ornamentation is inspired by nature. The flowers that were growing on the site before building work commenced, tagetes patula, appear on the tiles covering the Façade. In the grounds there are also many European fan palms whose leaves acted as models to produce the grille that protected the property. Inside, the ceilings are decorated with cherry leaves and fruits and on the walls are plant motifs, as well as many paintings of birds.

Outstanding are the trompes l'oeil, painted by Torrescassana, which maintain the garden atmosphere on the inside.

An interesting detail are the inscriptions which Gaudí ordered to be engraved on the frieze of the dining room gallery: Oh sombra de l'estiu [Oh shadow of summer] Sol solet vinam a veure [Little sun, come and see me] De la llart lo foch, visca lo foch de l'amor [From the home the fire, long live the fire of love]. The use of inscriptions would become a constant thread in the architect's work.

In 1925 the house was bought by a new owner who made important reforms. The work, for which Gaudí gave his consent, was entrusted to the architect Juan Bautista Serra de Martínez. The living space was doubled, respecting the volume and outside forms, the fountain was eliminated and the wooden oriental parasols were replaced by stained glass windows.

After the reform, in 1927 the Casa Vicens received the prize for the best building awarded by the City Council. In 1946 and 1962, the grounds where the waterfall and shrine devoted to Santa Rita were located were built on. Part of the grille was taken down and is today the gateway of Park Güell.

Casa Vicens before the mutilation of the garden.

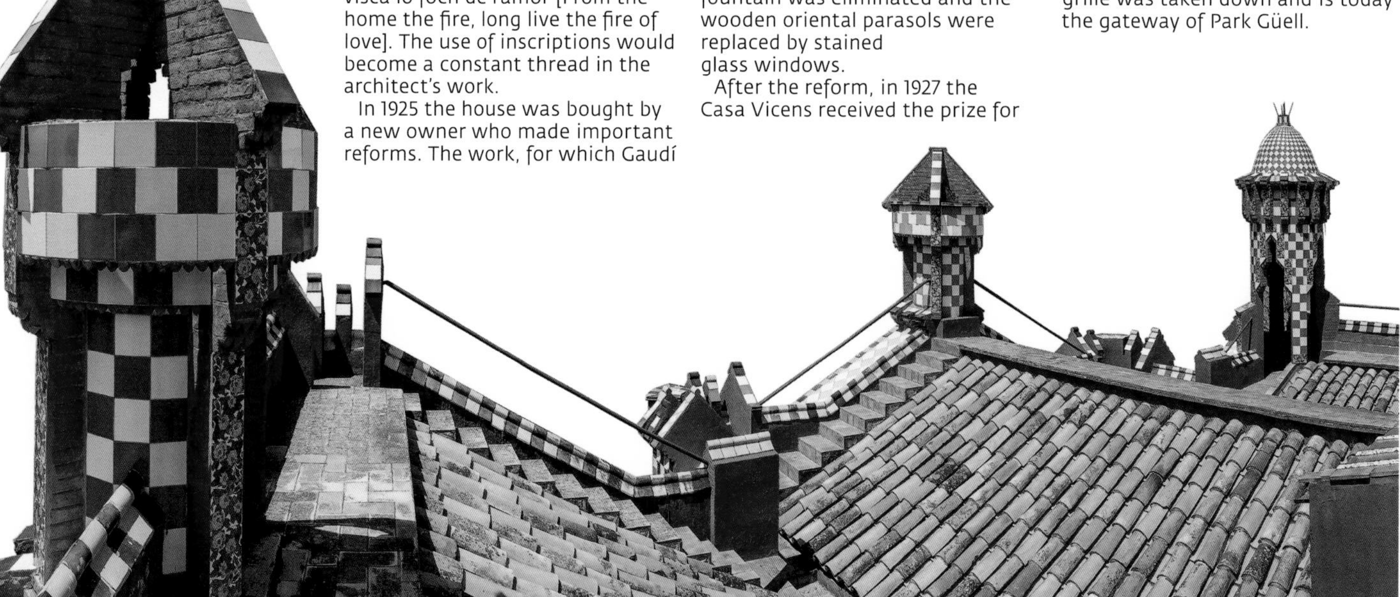

Roof with the ornamental tops and a type of walkway.

The treatment of the angles of the building enlivens a façade in which the flat surfaces still predominate.

Casa Vicens

1883-1888

Isolated residential building built as a summer residence.

It is structured on four levels: basement, ground floor and two upper floors, used as a storage area, living quarters, bedrooms and servant quarters, respectively.

The house has everything it needs for summer comfort, such as excellent ventilation on the inside and a large garden which originally included an artificial waterfall and the popular Santa Rita fountain, both demolished when the garden was dug up to make room for new constructions.

Considered as being Gaudí's first important piece of work, it is designed with great constructive simplicity, with a dominance of the straight line over the curve and with a notable emphasis of Arab-inspired aspects, such as the interior almocárabes, an interlaced design in plaster, and the outside solid brickwork.

The building is constructed of solid masonry walls, the floors with bricked up vaulting in their lowest part and with wooden beams on the higher floors and roofing.

Among the decorative work features the colourist ceramic covering on the Façades, which reproduce the flora of the site alternating between white and green tiles, as well as the decoration of the gallery that opens out to the garden, the smoking room and the dining room, for which Gaudí designed part of the furnishings.

Registered in the Catalogue of Historic and Artistic Architectural Heritage of Barcelona. National Heritage Site since 1969. UNESCO World Heritage Site

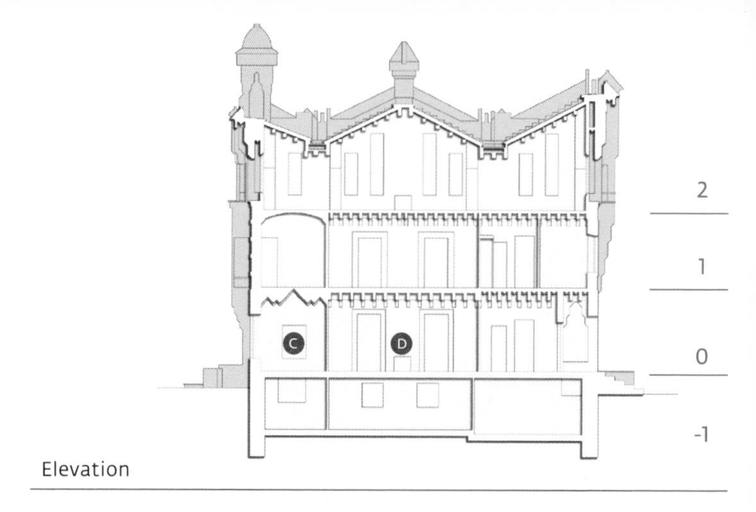

Elevation

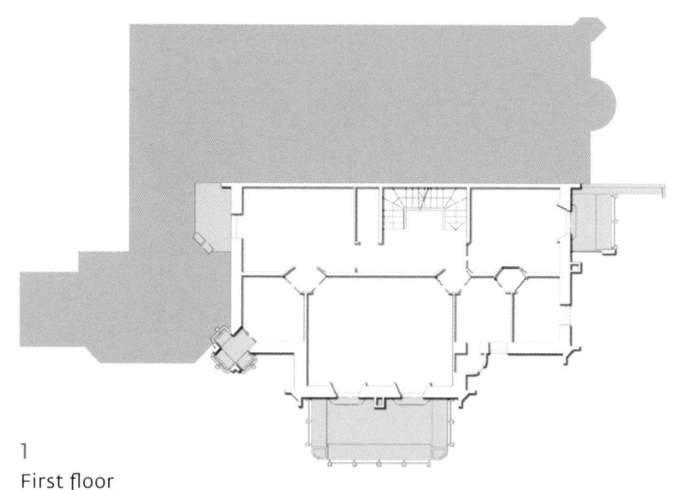

1
First floor

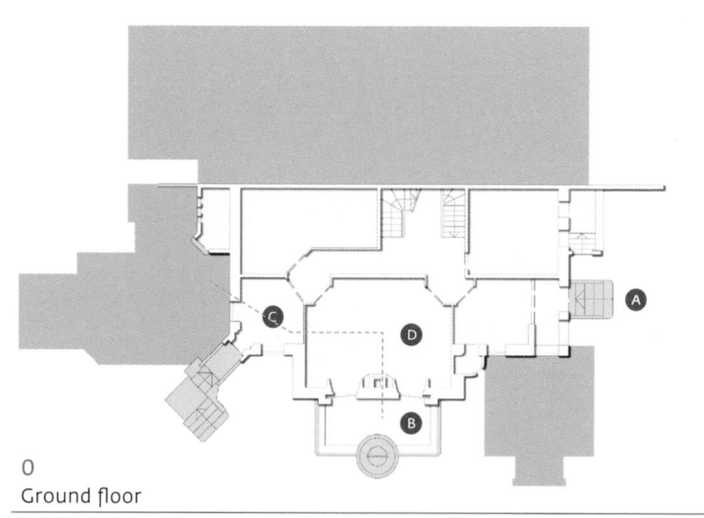

0
Ground floor

French marigold (*Tagetes patula*) on the tiles of the façade.

Casa Vicens
Manuel Vicens Montaner, promoter
20th of February 1883, project
1883-1888, construction
Collaborators:
Llorenç Matamala (sculptor)
Francesc Torrescassana (painter), Joan Oños (iron worker)

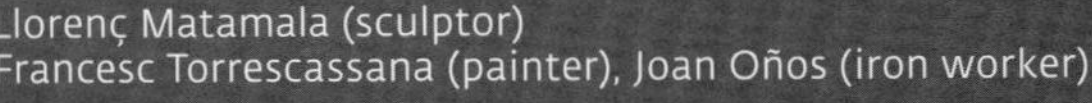

A Entrance
B Gallery
C Smoking room
D Dining room

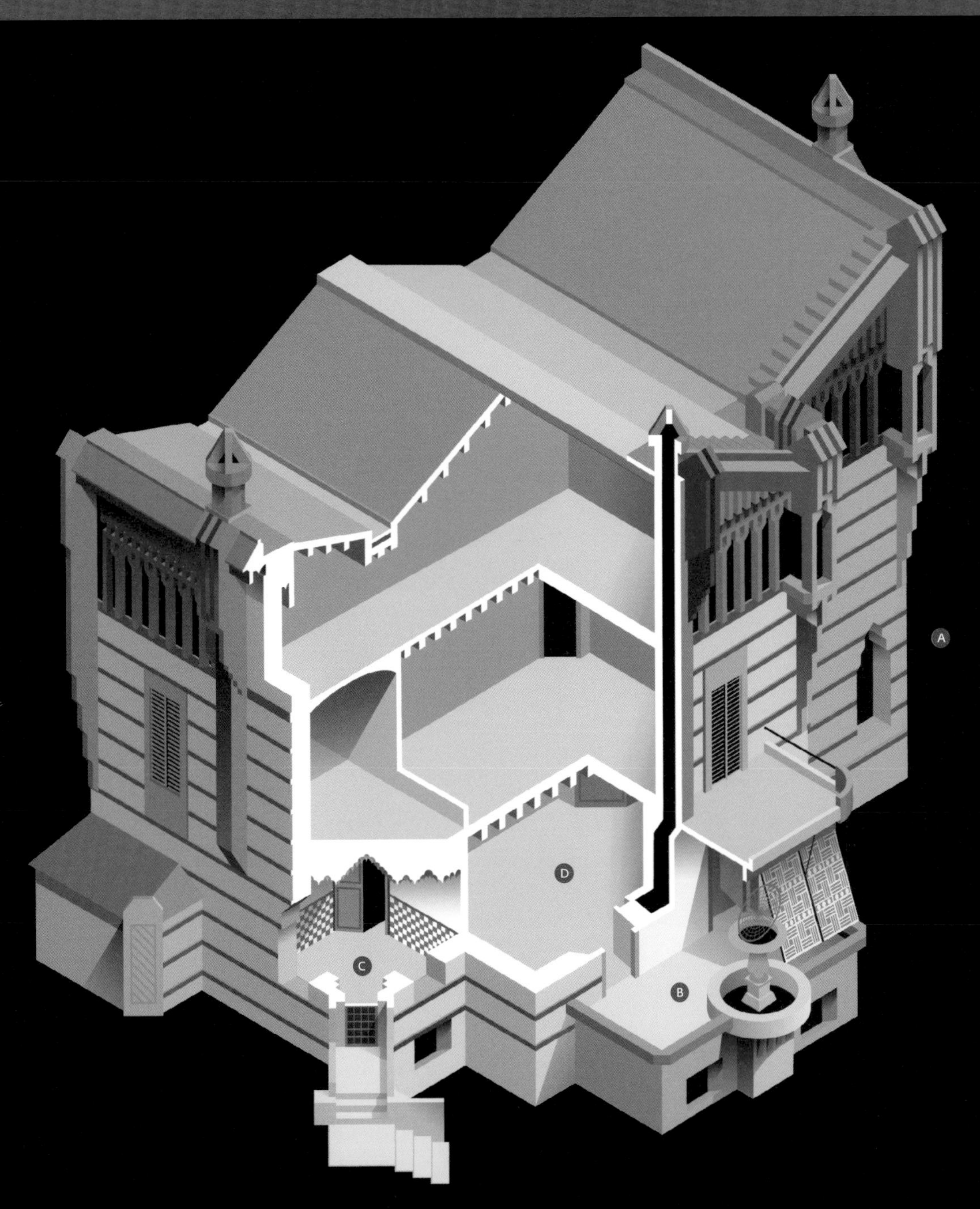

Entrance with the tiles with French marigold. Gaudí used this motif inspired by those that grew on the estate.

Part of the room that leads to the gallery in which one can appreciate the mural paintings.

Fumoir in arabised style.

Detail of the ceiling of the *fumoir*.

Shutter on one of the doors that leads to the garden.

Trompe-l'oeil on the ceiling of one of the rooms on the first floor.

El Capricho Villa Quijano

Comillas **Land on the Palacio de Sobrellano**

El Capricho

1883-1885

A royal visit

In 1881, Alfonso XII, king of Spain, stated his wish to spend the summer in Comillas, a village nearby Santander. The monarch was put up by Antonio López, a wealthy sea trader who, in 1878, had been awarded the title of Marquis of Comillas in payment for his determined defence of Spanish colonial interests in America.

In 1871, the marriage of Eusebi Güell, the most important member of the Catalan industrial elite, to Isabel López Bru, daughter of the marquis, had joined these two families, and they saw the king's visit as an unrepeatable opportunity to consolidate their position in the Spanish political scene. Nevertheless, the marquis was a member of the nouveau riche who possessed no ancestral property in which he could accommodate the monarch and the creation of a stately residence became of the utmost importance. To do this, Antonio López hired a group of leading Catalan architects – Domènech i Montaner, Cristóbal Cascante and Joan Martorell among others – who designed all kinds of monumental constructions.

The resources arriving from Barcelona meant that a flamboyant setting took form in which the artists and architects laid the basis for a new aesthetic to be born. The oriental-style constructions and the gardens illuminated by electric light – used for the first time in Spain – made up an exotic and rather extravagant atmosphere in which the bourgeoisie and nobility frivolously entertained themselves interpreting scenes from the Arabian Nights.

Within this context, Gaudí created a bandstand to celebrate the royal visit of 1881 and two years later built El Capricho, a retreat villa for Claudio López's brother-in-law, Máximo Díaz de Quijano. This piece of work maintains the references to Arab architecture begun in the Casa Vicens – the projections, the staggered windows, the brickwork, the glazed ceramic tiling and the courtyard – but there is an evolution present here in comparison.

In El Capricho, the angles disappear to be replaced by a space dominated by a curved line and the general appearance is more cheerful and light-hearted, thanks to the living presence of colour.

This particular building marked the beginning of themes and solutions that Gaudí would develop in later work: the watchtower, the most characteristic feature of the villa, is an architectural precedent that we come across later in Bellesguard and Park Güell. The on-site work was led by Cascante Colón, Gaudí's assistant.

Temporary kiosk that Gaudí designed for the visit to the estate by King Alfonso XII in 1891.

Capital of the columns of the entrance porch.

The tower, almost a minaret, is the part the most defines El Capricho.

El Capricho

1883-1885

A detached summerhouse built on a long, narrow, sloping site. Gaudí encountered the difficult task of starting the project from Barcelona and without having set foot on the site. Despite this setback, he decided on a long building, taking advantage of the gradient to include three spaces: a half-basement used as a garage and storeroom, a ground floor for the owner's home and an attic for the servants.

After the four single columns of the house which make up the entrance porch, he placed the front door, situated on the highest side of the building and over which he built a slender watch tower overlooking the sea.

To break with the long and monotonous site, Gaudí designed the main Façade with several projections, thus emphasising its rhythm. He built the lower part of the building with stone and the rest with open brickwork, which he covered on the outside with glazed ceramic leaves and flowers of different colours.

Gaudí was also commissioned to develop the surrounding area, designing a garden with several paths and a grotto.

As years passed by, the building was abandoned and suffered a great deal of damage until 1988, when it was restored by its owners. Today it houses a restaurant. Heritage Site since 1969.

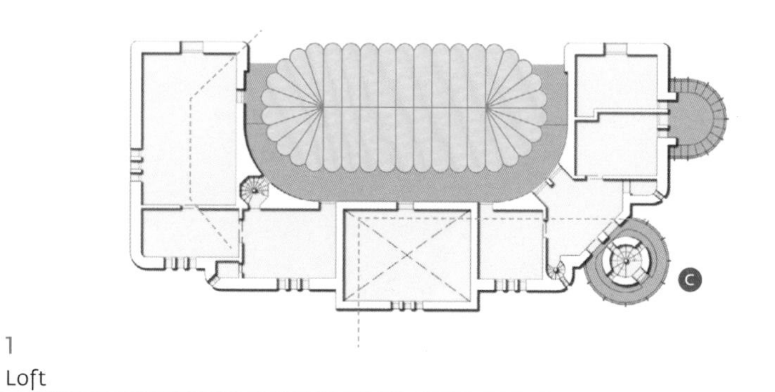

1

Loft

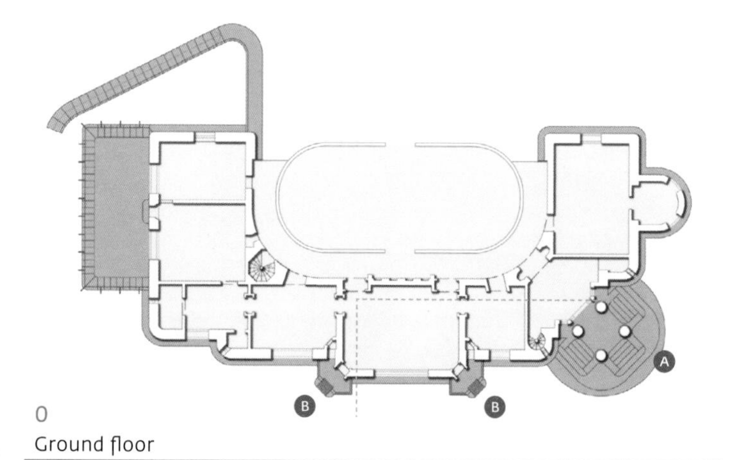

0

Ground floor

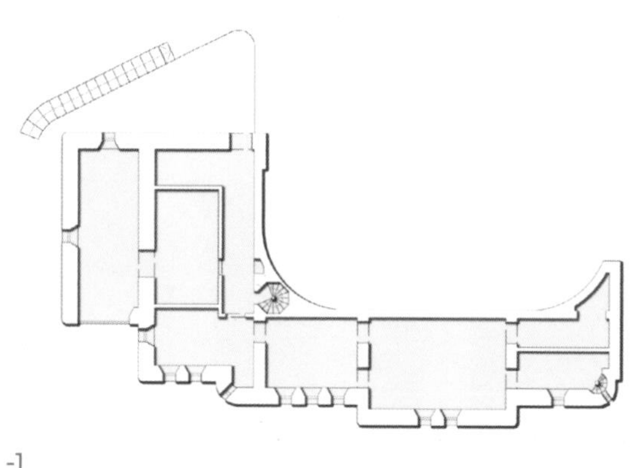

-1

Lower ground floor

Coffered ceiling on the ground floor.

El Capricho (Villa Quijano)
Máximo Díaz de Quijano, promoter
1883-1885, construction
Collaborators:
Cristòfol Cascante, Camil Oliveras (architects)

A Entrance
B Balcony
C Tower

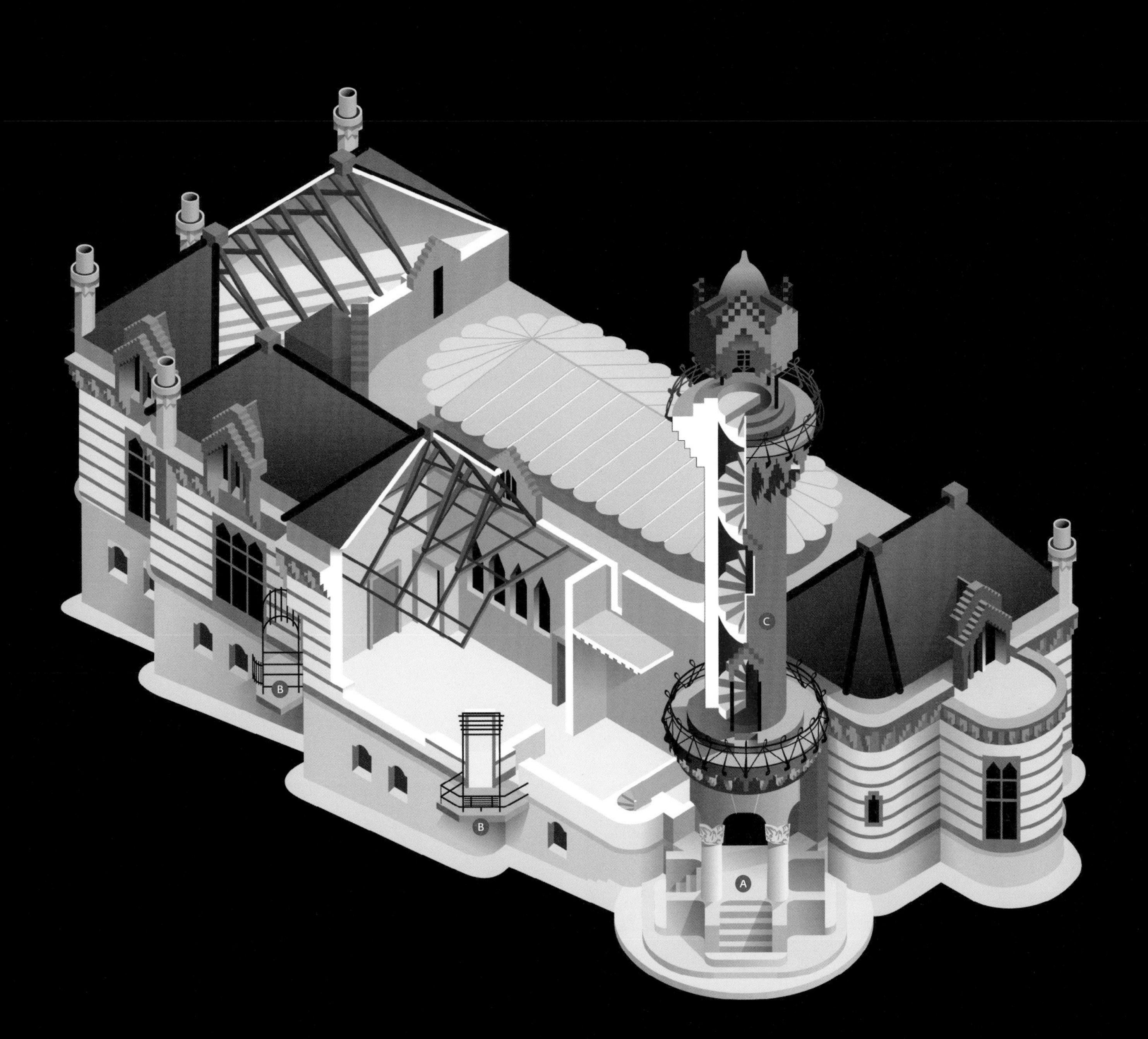

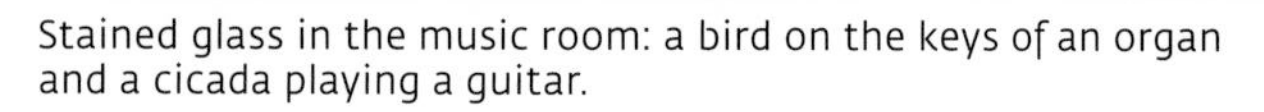

Stained glass in the music room: a bird on the keys of an organ and a cicada playing a guitar.

Ornamental top of the cast iron of the viewpoint.

Loft door that leads to the balcony.

Gaudí designed a bench integrated into the balcony railing.

Detail of the corbels beneath the bench-balcony.

Ceiling of the loft.

Stained glass of the lobby.

Base of a column of the porch.

Entrance porch above which rises the tower-viewpoint.

Ornamental top of the tower-viewpoint.

Brickwork is also combined with the sunflower ceramics on the outside wall.

Güell pavilions

Pavellons Güell

Barcelona Avinguda de Pedralbes, 7

1

Pavellons Güell

1884-1887

The Garden of the Hesperides

Joan Güell Ferrer bought the area that today makes up Pedralbes, two large estates with beautiful gardens surrounding an 18th century house, in the town of Les Corts. For this spot, the Güell family commissioned Gaudí to build, among other minor tasks, the pavilions making up the lodge house and stables. The Güell pavilions are the clearest example of Gaudí's treatment of medieval Mudejar architecture. Nevertheless, this is not merely a historical imitation of this style but a new interpretation that combines the past with the infant modernism.

This construction begins to reveal Gaudí's interest in crowning elements and the itineraries taken over the roofing that would become one of the characteristics of his work.

The relationship with literature was very common in the architecture of that period and in the case of the pavilions there is a close link with the poetic universe of Jacint Verdaguer. The mythical world that appears as a background to the pavilions is that of Atlantis, an epic poem that tells how Hercules robbed the golden fruit from the garden of the Hesperides guarded by Ladon, represented by the extraordinary cast iron dragon. The abundant iconography of the pavilions includes elements such as the lyre of the grilles, the antimony orange tree, representing the mythical tree of the Hesperides, the G anagrams of Güell, or the sculpted flowers on the pillars supporting the iron grille which represent the eglantine, the wild rose handed over to the winning poets of the "Floral Games", the poetry competition won by Verdaguer in 1877. The poet baptised the estate with the name of "Torre Satalia", referring to a variety of wild rose.

Today, the old stables house the headquarters of the Gaudí Centre.

Postcard produced in 1905.

A sculpture of Hercules, no longer there, crowned the fountain in allusion to the episode of the garden of the Hesperides.

Spout of the Hercules fountain in the form of a dragon.

Roofing of the stables.

Pavellons Güell

1884-1887

A set of two auxiliary constructions, one designed as stables and exercise ring for horses, and the other as a lodge and dwelling for the caretaker.

The first was built with just a ground floor plan and with access to the flat roof, whereas the second building has a ground and first floor, integrating both the workspace and the accommodation into a single building.

The structure of the two buildings is based on load-bearing walls, vaulting and parabolic arches. Gaudí used brick as the basic construction material and in some parts applied, for the first time, the ceramic *trencadís* mosaic, the practical system for outdoor covering made from broken tiles that are adapted to curved surfaces. Both pavilions bring to mind the aesthetic style present in his other contemporary buildings, as well as the predominance of the straight line over the curve.

Outside, the marked volume of the horizontal is crowned by several lanterns which, from the roofs, light up the interior vaulting through which the light is reflected.

In between the two buildings a spectacular wrought-iron gate stands out, cast in 1885 in the Barcelona workshop of Vallet y Piqué, and which represents a dragon, the immortal watchman of the property.

On the death of Eusebi Güell in 1918, the heirs separated the estate, being split up further in 1924 with the opening of Avenida Diagonal. The perimeter closure wall was demolished and the other two auxiliary doors through which the property was entered thus lost their function.

National Heritage Site since 1969.

Secondary door of the estate.

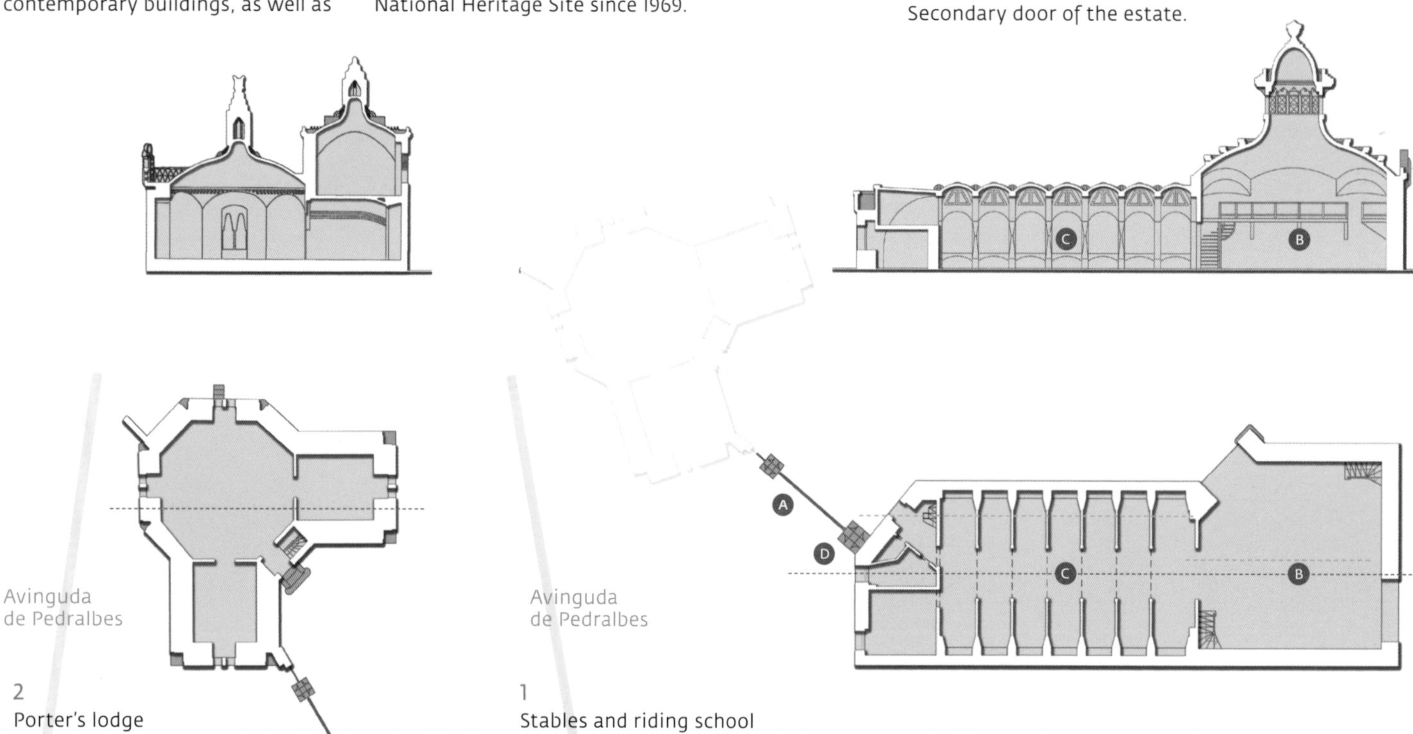

2
Porter's lodge

1
Stables and riding school

Güell pavilions
Eusebi Güell i Bacigalupi, promoter
1884-1887, project and construction
Collaborators:
Vallet i Piqué Workshops (iron workers)

(A) Wrought-iron door
(B) Riding school
(C) Stables
(D) Orange tree

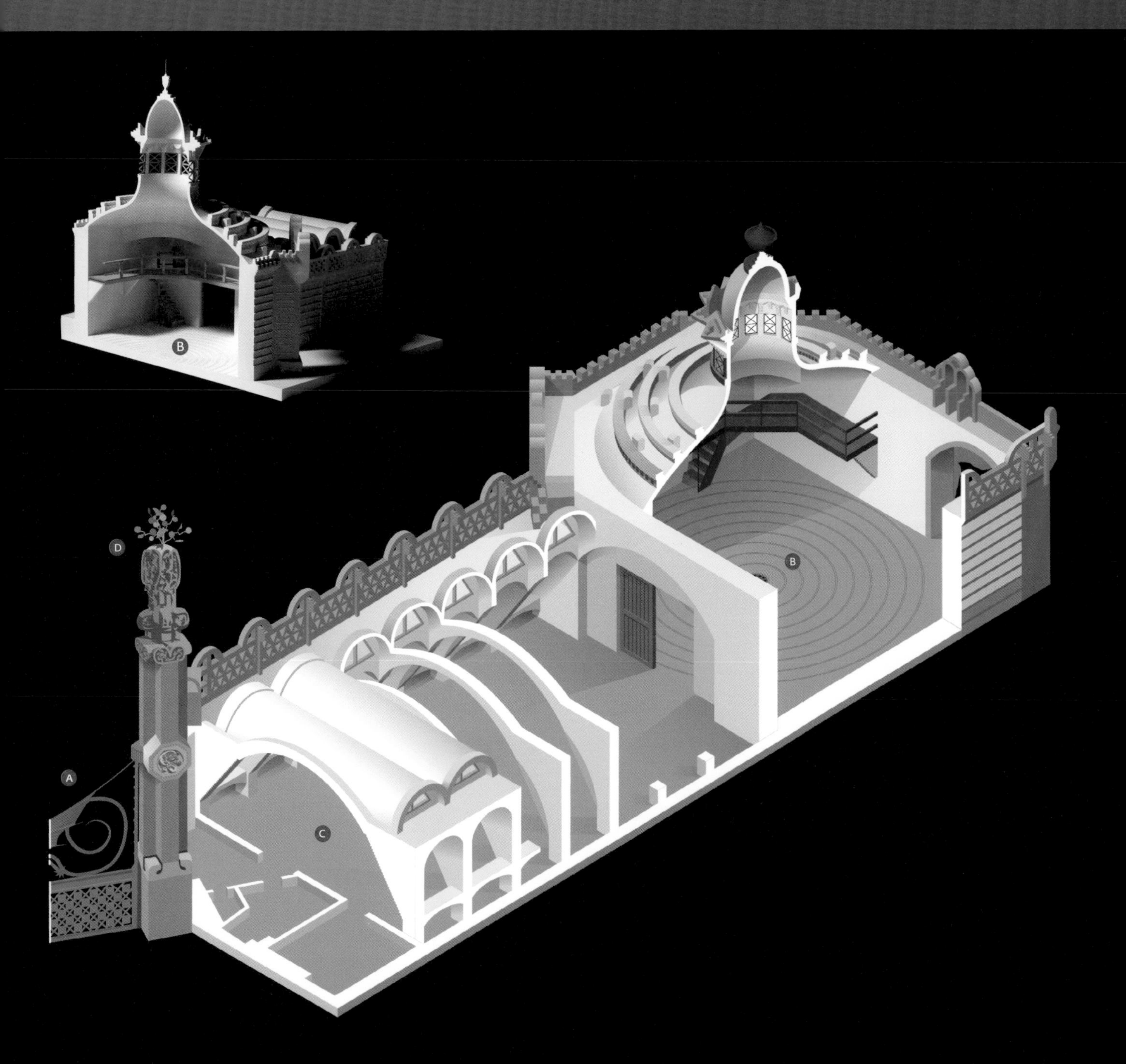

The entrance gate has two openings, a small one for pedestrians with the grille crowned by the lyre, and the larger one, for carriages, with the famous dragon. The pavilion on the left was the porter's lodge and the one on the right, the stables and riding school.

Head of the wrought iron dragon on the door for carriages.

Antimony orange tree over the pillar of the entrance door, with the golden fruits of the Hesperides that the dragon protected.

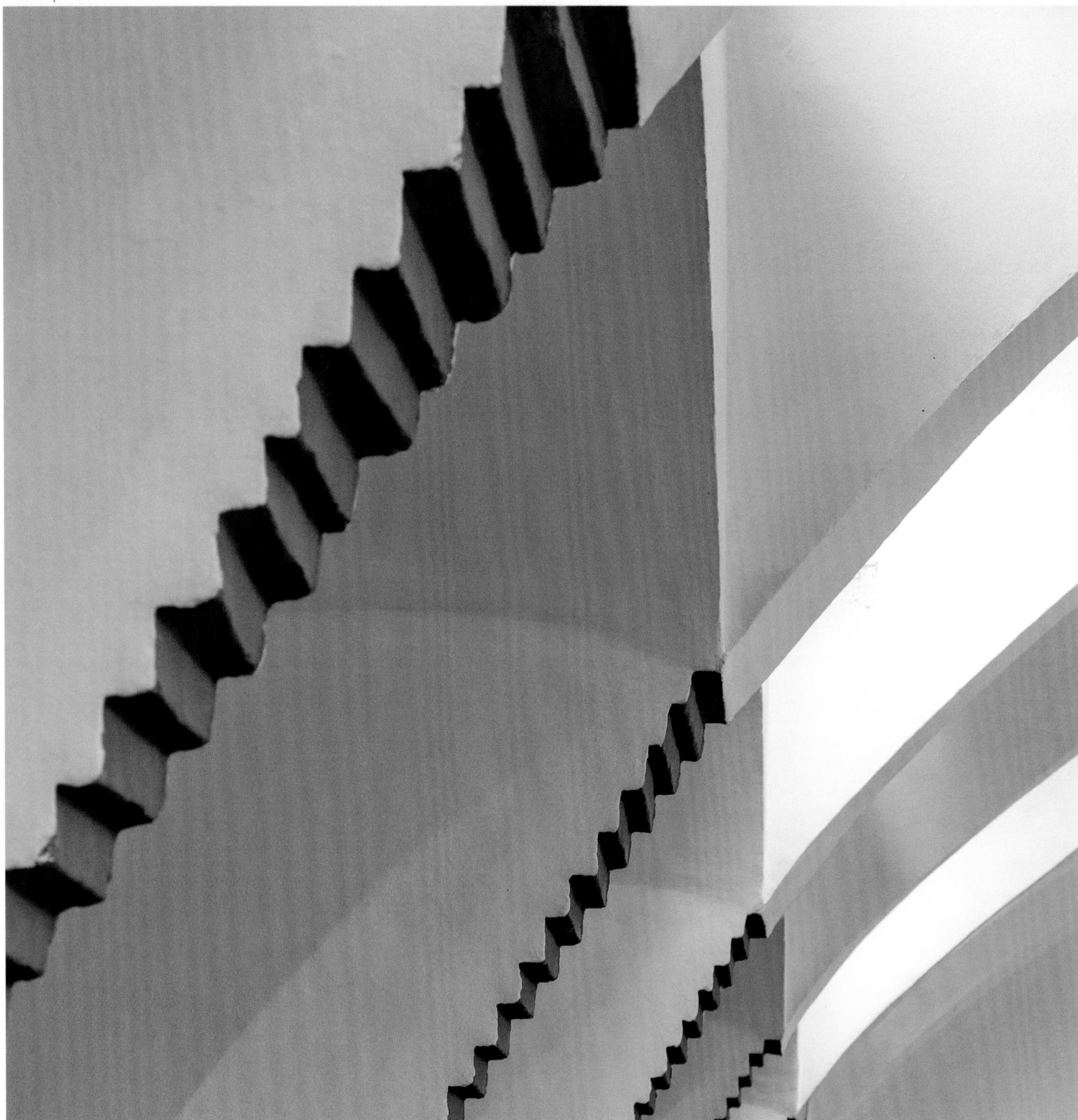

Detail of the origin of the parabolic arches.

Parabolic arches of the old stables.

Cast iron lyre (homage to the poet Jacint Verdaguer) that crowns the top of the iron gate of the pedestrian entrance.

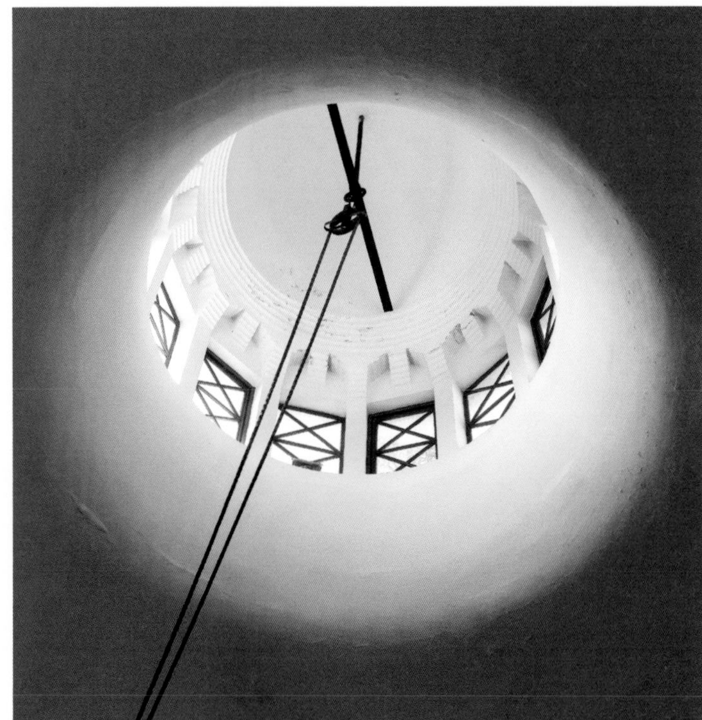

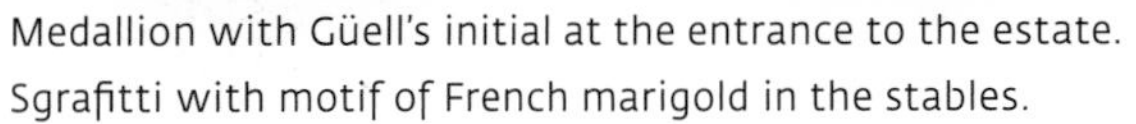

Medallion with Güell's initial at the entrance to the estate.

Sgrafitti with motif of French marigold in the stables.

Lantern of the riding school.

The G of Güell on the floor of the riding school.

Palau Güell

Barcelona Carrer Nou de la Rambla, 3-5

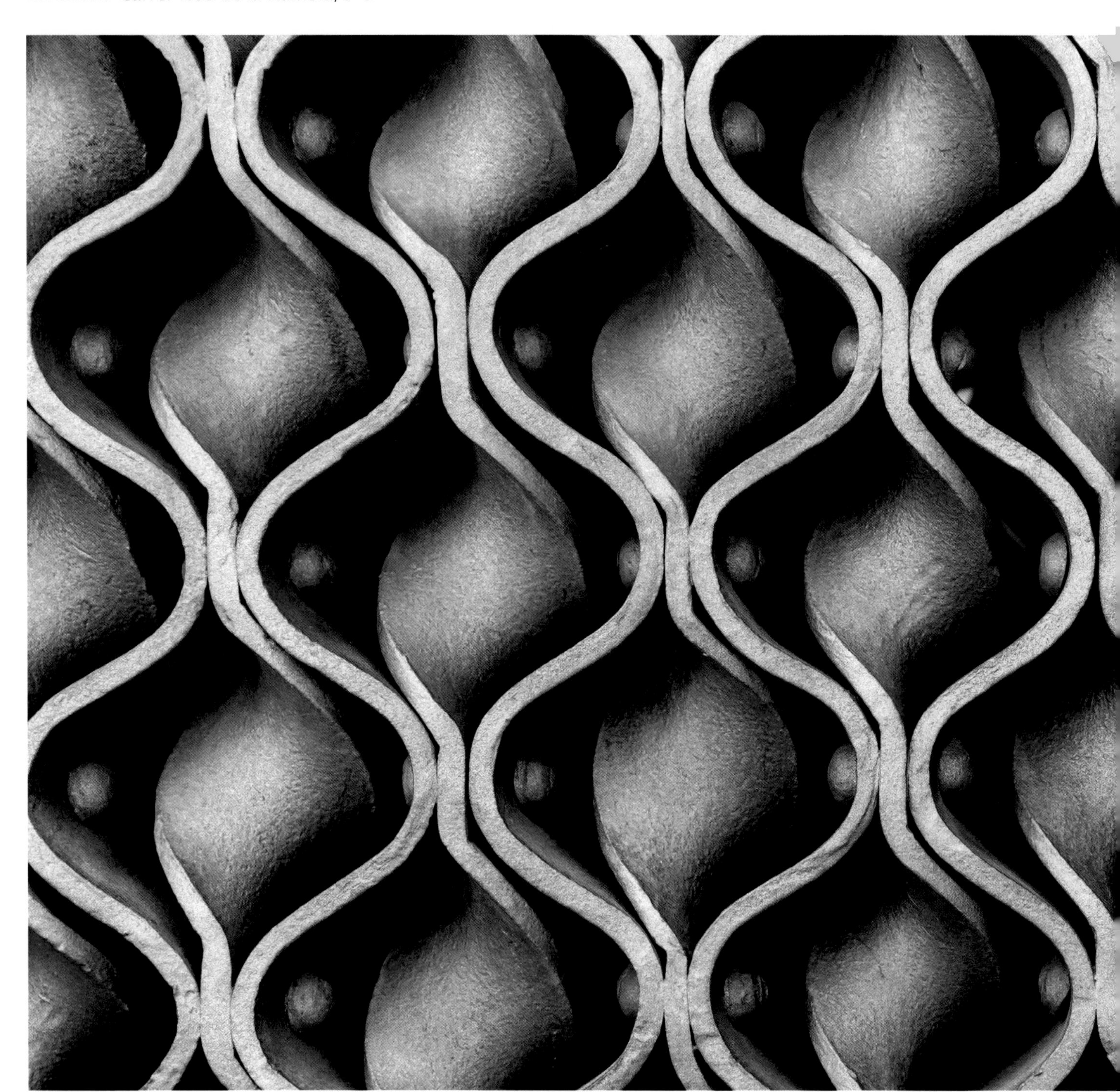

2

Palau Güell

1886-1888

A palace for the Barcelona bourgeoisie

In 1886, Eusebi Güell commissioned Antoni Gaudí to build a stately home in Carrer Nou de la Rambla. In the report of 1886 with which the Development Commission gave its permission, originally denied by the City Council, to build the Güell Palace, it is described in the following way: "Even though it does not boast of a having a monumental aspect, it does at least have a certain richness, magnificence and suchlike details, and there will be few in the enlarged district of the city that will be able to compete with it".

For the first time, Gaudí converted a structural element, the catenary arch, into an ornament that served as an entrance door into the palace. The imposing marble Façade – for which Gaudí produced more than 20 different projects – had a great impact on the Barcelona of that time and the building provoked all kinds of comments. Santiago Rusiñol, with a certain amount of irony, classified the palace as "Babylonic" and an anecdote tells the story of two passers-by passing before the palace, exclaiming, "what a weird and strange thing". On hearing this, Güell said to Gaudí, "I like it more now", since the patron, of humble beginnings, found in art a way of showing off his new social position. His coat of arms, designed by Gaudí, contains a motto taken from a verse by Verdaguer: "ahir pastor, avui senyor" [Yesterday shepherd, today lord]. The main hall, covered by a very high cupola that rises above the flat roof, was the setting for concerts and theatrical productions and one of the meeting points for the Barcelona bourgeoisie.

Behind an ordered and austere outside appearance, the structuralisation of the indoor spaces is the palace's greatest achievement. The building represents the continuation of the experiment begun in the pavilions with the crowning elements of the roof. The sober Façades contrast with the cheerful colouring of the chimneys. As regards the design, the palace shows how much of nineteenth-century influence remained in 1890. Light, one of the constant concerns of Gaudí's constructions, is filtered into the building through the many windows on the Façade and the holes in the central cupola.

During the Civil War, the palace was confiscated by the anarchists who used the basement as a prison. In 1944, an American was at the point of buying it to move it stone by stone to America. From 1945 onwards, the Barcelona Regional Council began work on the building's restoration. In 1971 a new restoration campaign was begun which went on until 1979. This intervention mainly involved the Façade and flat roof which was once again restored at the beginning of the nineties.

Postcard from the early 20th century (1910).

Phoenix bird over the coat of arms of Catalonia.

Catenary arches of the entrance.

Palau Güell

1886-1888

A family residence built in the historic centre of Barcelona and designed as an extension of another property owned by the Güell family in La Rambla and with which it was connected. It has six levels organised in different ways and for different purposes: the basement for stables, the ground floor for the reception, the mezzanine for the office, the first floor the home, the second floor the bedrooms and the third floor for the loft.

The basement features the helicoid ramp for the horses and the thick brick pillars which, together with the load-bearing walls, support the weight of the building. Of the rest of the building, mention must be made of its architectural conception, based on a very well lit central hall of over 80 m² and 17 m high, around which all the different rooms are positioned. The space is closed by a cupola, produced by a revolving paraboloid, which is covered with marble plaques full of holes allowing the light to filter through and resulting in an interesting luminous effect.

Gaudí used the parabolic arch, a geometric shape that appears constantly in all his later work, to a great extent and covered the ceilings of many rooms with wooden coffers, some worked with metallic elements with which they formed both decoration and structure. He also designed several functional elements, such as the flat roof chimneys, and took great care in working the materials well, such as the cast iron entrance doors that include the owner's initials on their upper section. Gaudí took full advantage of material that came from the owner's properties, such as the stone from Garraf with which the property's Façades were built. The architect was also commissioned to design furniture, lights and stained glass windows, which he produced with the very best materials, ranging from delicate marbles to top quality woods, ceramics and multicoloured glass. With these materials he recreated atmospheres that were evocative of Gothic style and of Muslim art according to his own interpretation. He also made abundant use of the parabolic arch.

National Heritage Site since 1969. UNESCO World Heritage Site.

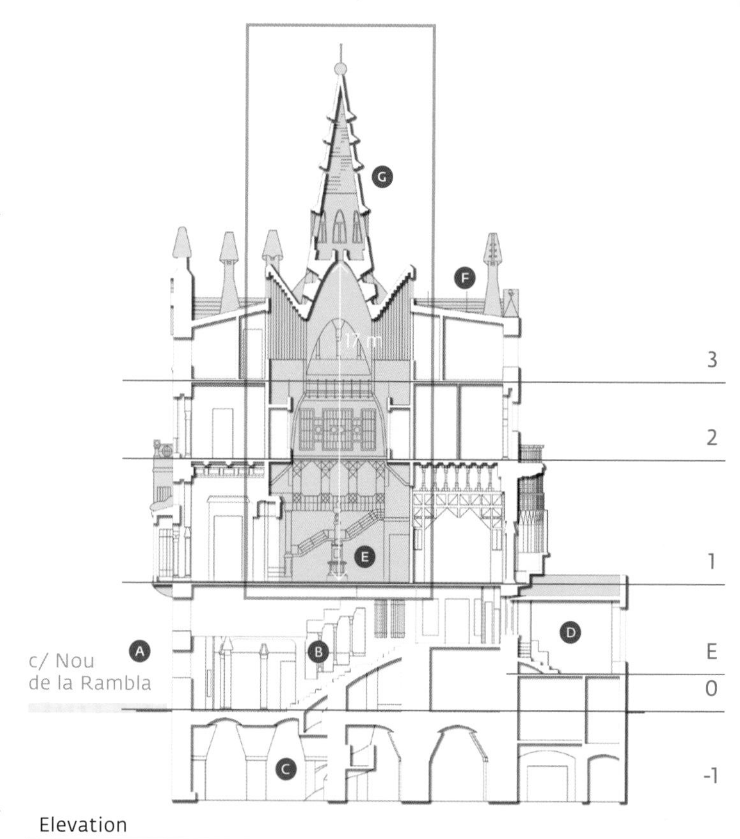

Elevation

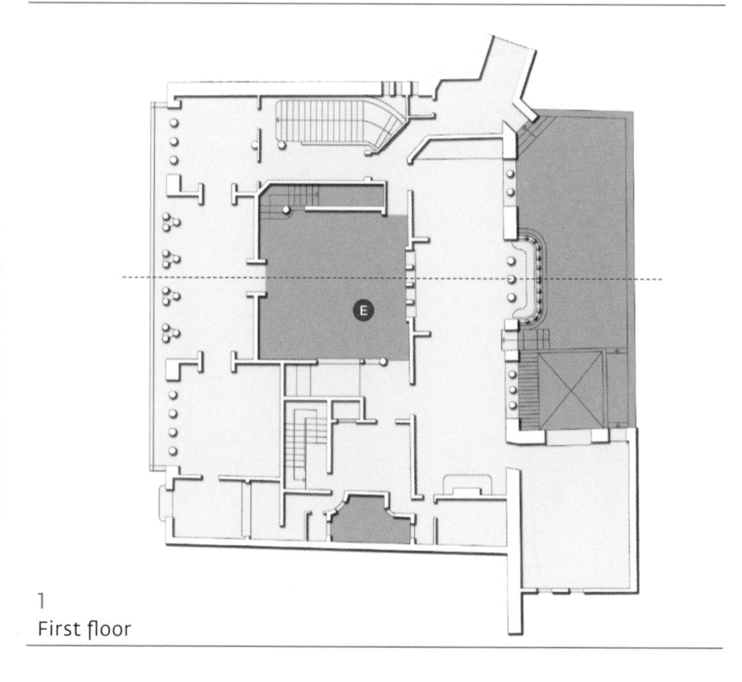

1
First floor

The wrought iron work of the entrance grilles are extraordinary and include the initials of Eusebi Güell. On the door on the right is the letter G.

Palau Güell
Eusebi Güell i Bacigalupi, promoter
30th of June 1886, project
1886-1888, construction
Collaborators:
Francesc Berenguer (architect)
Aleix Clapés (painter)
Camil Oliveras, Joan Oños,
J. Gabarró (iron workers)
Joan Soley, Eudaldo Puntí
(carpenters and cabinetmakers)
Ventura Hermanos (marble mason)
Antoni Oliva (decorator) Agustí
Masip (builder)

- A Entrance
- B Main stairway
- C Stables
- D Office
- E Lounge
- F Chimneys
- G Cupola

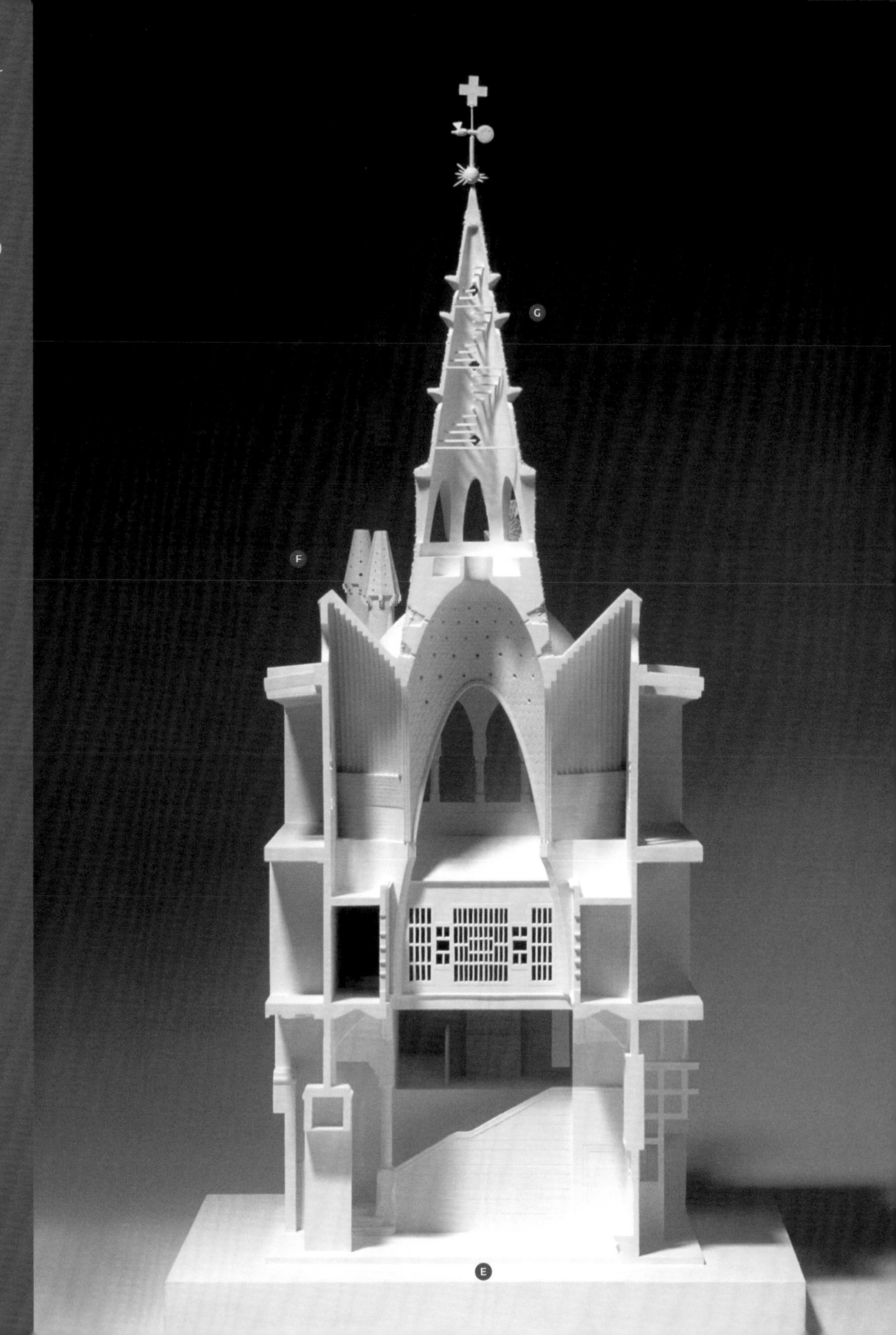

Marble stairway of the main entrance.

The entrance seen from the main stairway.

Spiral access to the stables.

Gaudí produced the stable space from thick brick columns
with fungiform capitals.

The main room, on the first floor, has a height of three floors, with an organ placed on the last one.

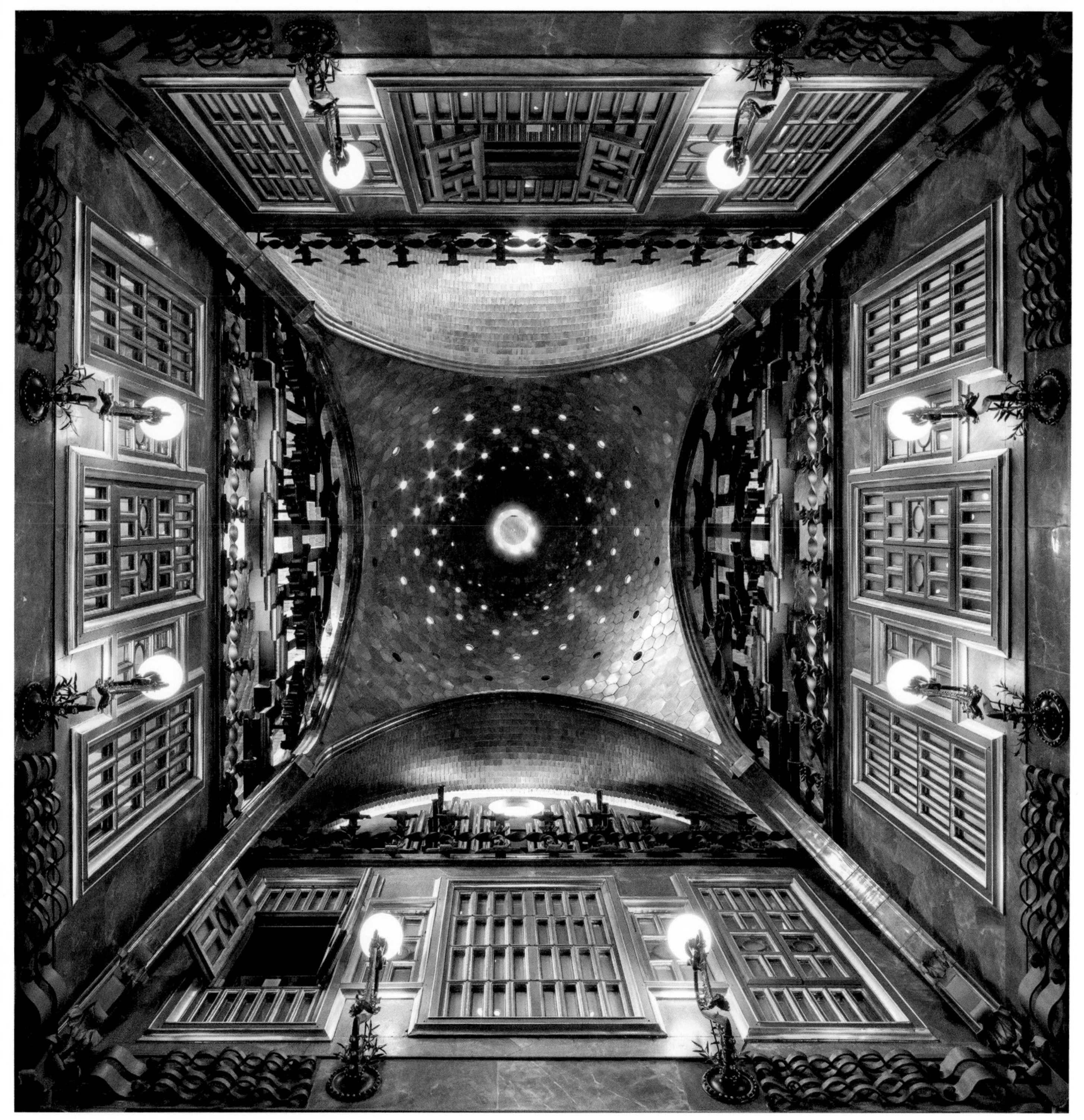

The dome of the room has hexagonal pieces perforated to let the outside light in. The whole complex is like a heavenly dome in which the stars shine brightly.

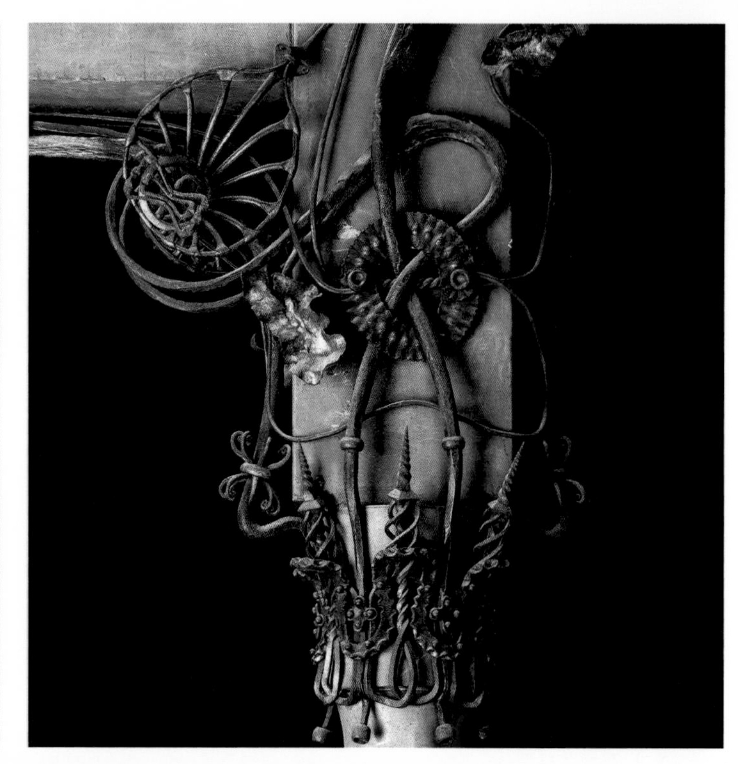

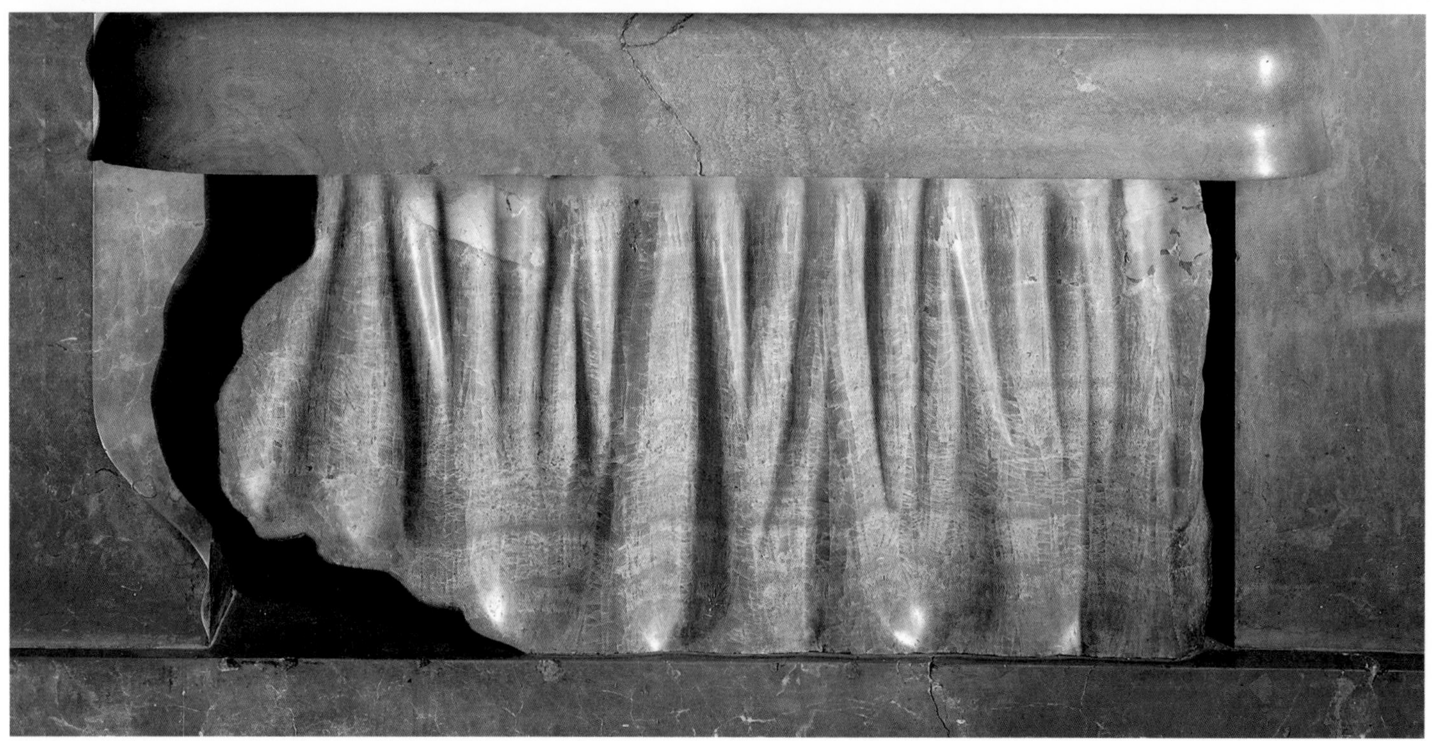

Details of the exquisite works of carpentry and wrought iron (above) and marble work (below).

Catenary arches on the top floor, that of the organ.

First scenic intervention by Gaudí on a flat roof, a precedent of what he would produce in Casa Batlló and La Pedrera.

Gaudí believed that buildings should be crowned with elements of great artistic power, whether they were chimneys, openings, ventilation ducts, etc.

On the flat roof, the lantern over the dome of the room has morphology similar to that of termites.

Theresan College

Col·legi de les Teresianes

Barcelona Carrer de Ganduxer, 85

Col·legi de les Teresianes
1888-1890

Mystical architecture

"The college will be highly adorned and strange or unique, in the style of Gaudí". These were the words with which Enric d'Ossó, founder of the order, defined this college built for the group of nuns of Saint Theresa and devoted to teaching in Spain, America and Africa.

The college had to be built in a short time and with a reduced budget, a fact that forced him to use a rational architectural language that would take the utmost advantage of the scarce resources. This explains the austere appearance of the building which, without losing a certain Mudejar air, is a long way off the picturesque style of Gaudí's early work.

Behind the secretiveness of the outer walls is an interior in which the light, the symbolic presence of God, penetrates the entire building, producing an intimate atmosphere of peace and shelter. In an architectural transliteration of the poetic message of Saint Theresa, the attainment of cloister arches results in an area of pure forms, showing the importance of the internal, the essence, contrasted to the external, the appearance.

Gaudí, who was an admirer of the mystical poetry of the Spanish Golden Age and of the poems of Saint Theresa of Ávila, decorated the building with Theresan symbols: the name of Jesus and fire, representing devotion, appear on the window grilles of the ground floor and between the merlons there are brick balusters and stained glass pieces, with the T of Saint Theresa. The entrance porch floor features the verse from one of the poems by Saint Theresa: "Everything passes".

The college at the end of the 19th century.

Theresan shield: Mount Carmelo crowned by the cross, with the star on its base and flanked by the hearts of Jesus and Therese.

Handle in the form of a T, the initial of the saint's name.

Main façade with the catenary arch entrance.

Col·legi de les Teresianes

1888-1890

A school building (convent, college and boarding school) begun in late-1888 by an unknown architect, it was shortly after entrusted to Gaudí, when the building was at the height of the second floor. Despite this factor imposing the ground plan on his work, rectangular and very long, he was able to complete the work in little less than a year after amending the original project substantially.

The Theresan College has four floors (ground floor plus three upper floors) designed as three longitudinal spaces, the central one being a skylight. With this system Gaudí achieved the entrance of light from the top floor through to the ground floor and which in its trajectory, lit up all the adjoining rooms.

He used the parabolic arch for both the outside and the inside. They stand out in the corridors that support the light well, forming spaces of remarkable architectural, aesthetic and luminescent resolution. The main materials he used were stone and solid brick, of a low cost but nevertheless very serious, contrasting with the elaborate wrought iron and ceramic work.

Gaudí was also commissioned to develop the surrounding area, designing a huge garden according to his own particular naturalist way of conceiving spaces, in which he planted palm trees and pines surrounding the paths and stone benches. The main part of the garden disappeared with the construction of the Barcelona Ring Road.

Although the Theresan College suffered a great deal of damage in 1936, when it was attacked and pillaged, it still continues functioning as an educational centre.

National Heritage Site since 1969.

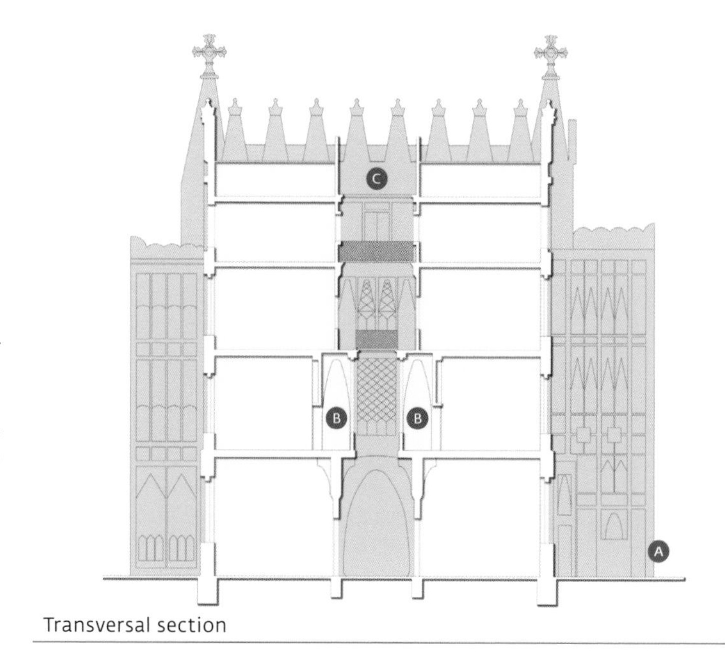

Transversal section

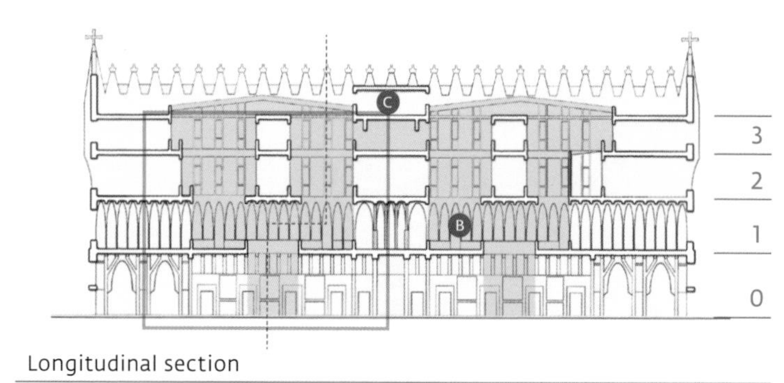

Longitudinal section

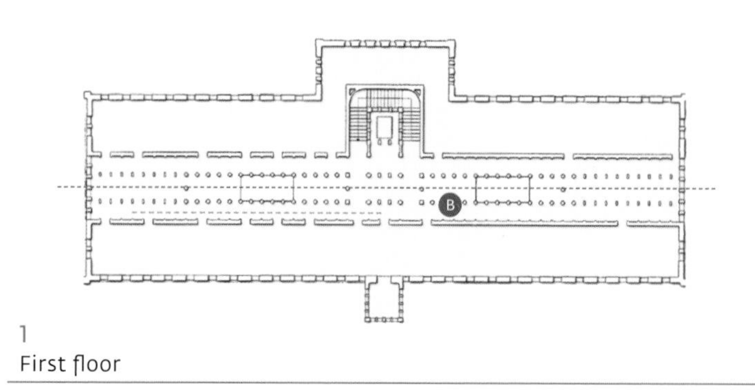

1
First floor

"All things pass", verse on the threshold of the entrance of the religious poem by Saint Therese *God alone is enough*: (...) Let nothing upset you / All things pass / (...) / God alone is enough.

Theresan College
Enric d'Ossó, Order of Saint Theresa, promoter
1888-1890, project and construction

- (A) Entrance
- (B) Gallery
- (C) Chandelier

The ironwork of the grille of the main entrance also reproduces the Theresan shield.

Catenary arches of the corridor on the ground floor.

Passage of the cloister on the first floor crowned with catenary arches
an in which one can appreciate the magnificent distribution of the light.

The Theresan shields, as well as the battlements of the building, are crowned by a mortarboard, a symbol of the saint, since she was the first doctor of the Catholic Church. The pinnacles of the angles, in contrast, are crowned by a four-armed cross.

Episcopal Palace of Astorga

Palacio Episcopal de Astorga

Astorga **Plaza de Eduardo Castro**

EPISCOPI AEDIBVS. PALATIVM
CONSVMPTIS

Palacio Episcopal de Astorga

1889-1893

A neo-gothic palace

In 1886, when a fire destroyed the diocesan headquarters of Astorga, Joan Grau Vallespinós held the post of Bishop of the town. After several frustrated attempts to commission a local architect, the bishop recommended his friend Gaudí. In June 1889, after two years of interminable bureaucratic wrangling, the first stone of the Episcopal palace was laid.

The architect was unable to lead the project personally due to commitments he had in Barcelona but he conceived it and made an exhaustive monitoring of the progress of the works with photographs. Nevertheless, he was able to make occasional trips to Astorga and took advantage of his stays to make some change or other in the design aspects of the palace and to deepen further his friendship with Grau who, it seems, had a profound influence on Gaudí's religious outlook.

In 1893 bishop Grau died, and Gaudí, at loggerheads with the Diocesan Council due to differences of opinion, handed in his resignation in the same year. On leaving he remarked, "They will not be able to finish it or to leave it interrupted". The palace was unfinished without the roofing. In 1905 the new bishop of Astorga, Julian de Diego Alcolea, tried to convince Gaudí to finish the work, but Gaudí refused.

After the sporadic involvement of several architects, the palace was completed between 1907 and 1924 under the direction of Ricardo García Guereta. The zinc angels, designed by Gaudí, should have crowned the building but were not finally placed on pedestals at the foot of the building until 1963.

Photograph from 1927.

The zinc angels carry some of the attributes of the bishops such as the mitre or the staff.

Gaudí used local materials such as slate or granite from Bierzo.

Palacio Episcopal de Astorga

1889-1893

Detached building constructed in a particular Gothic style and very much in harmony with the local architecture. It has four levels: the lower-ground floor (for the archive and storeroom), the ground floor (that includes the vestibule, reception, conference room, secretary's office, several offices and the notaries' and clerks' rooms), the first floor (for the chapel, the throne room, dining room, library, the bishop's private quarters and several bedrooms for guests) and the attic (for the servants).

The palace is built around load-bearing walls and columns, and features the abundant use of flat brick ogival and rib vaulting, the type of vaulting dominant throughout the building.

An outstanding feature of the exterior is the entrance portico, whose voussoirs, enlarged in the form of a fan, frame the three entrance doors. Also dominant are the sober stone walls, the many windows, the circular towers and the wide ditch surrounding the building, enabling light to enter the basement and through which the three service doors can be reached.

Museum of the Ways since 1963. Heritage Site since 1969. Integral part of the Road to Santiago since 1999.

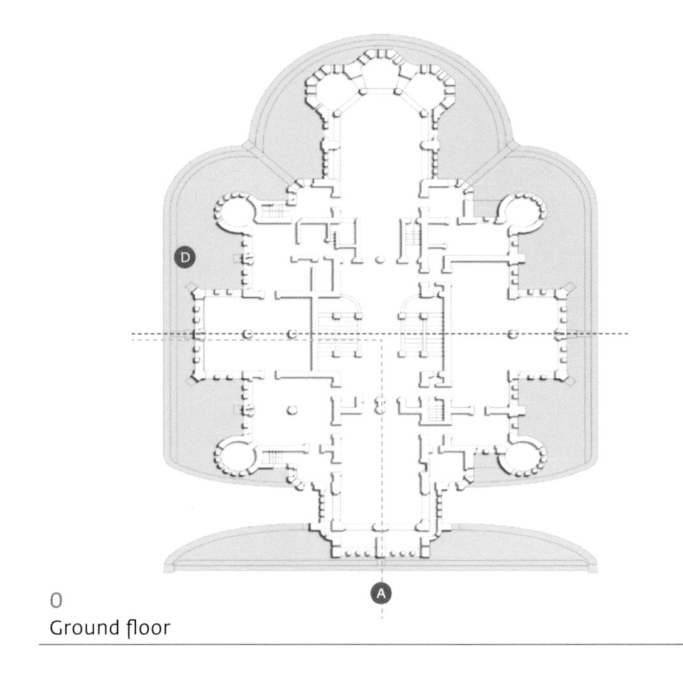

0
Ground floor

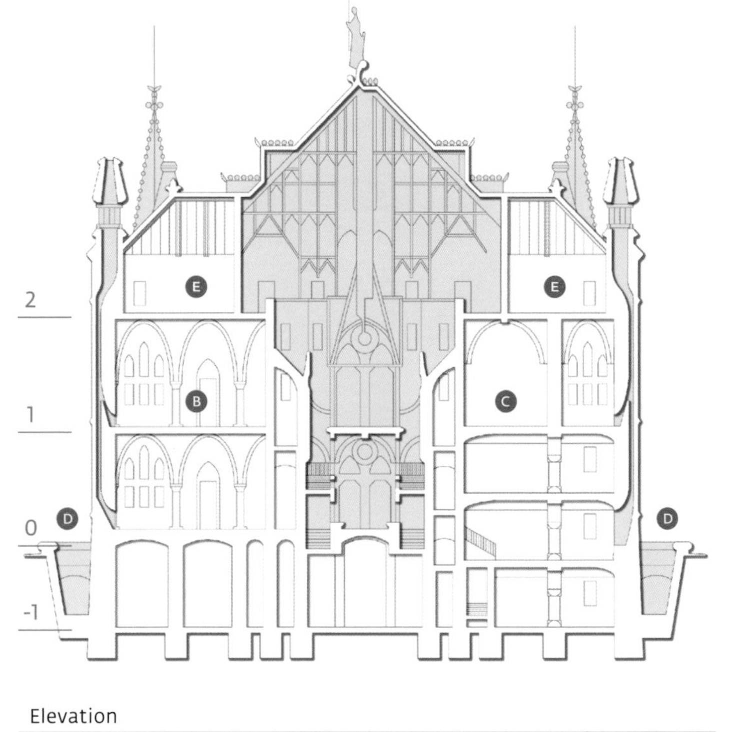

Elevation

The ribbing of the cross vaults is made of local ceramics, specifically from Jiménez de Jamuz.

Episcopal Palace of Astorga
Joan Bautista Grau Vallespinos, promoter
August 1887, project
1889-1893, construction

- (A) Entrance
- (B) Library
- (C) Lounge
- (D) Moat
- (E) Loft

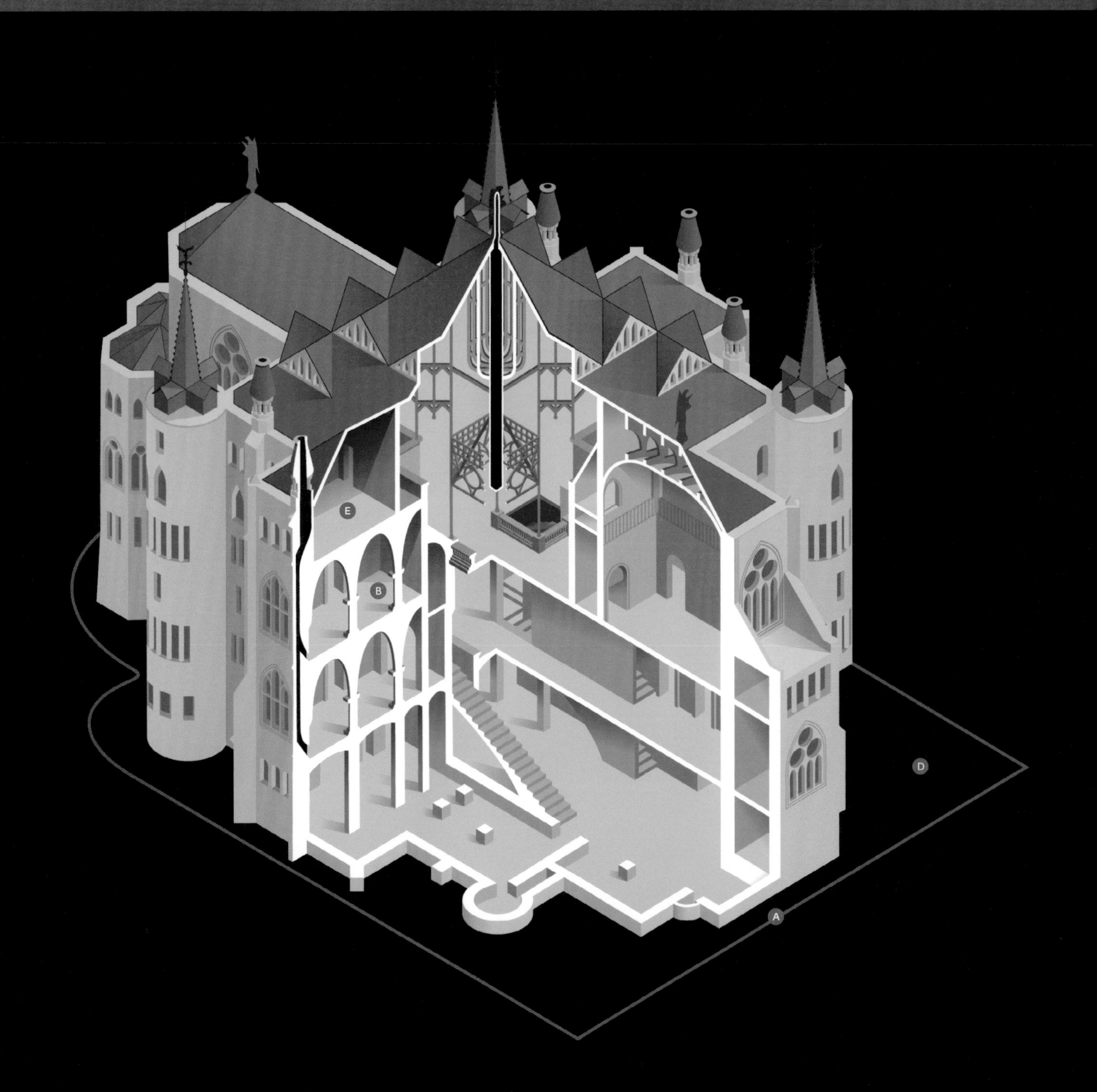

Three large trumpet-shaped arches give originality to the entrance porch.

Former dormitory of the bishop. Stone, ceramic and glass combine in a well-lit and cosy space.

Casa Botines Casa Fernández y Andrés

León Plaza de San Marcelo

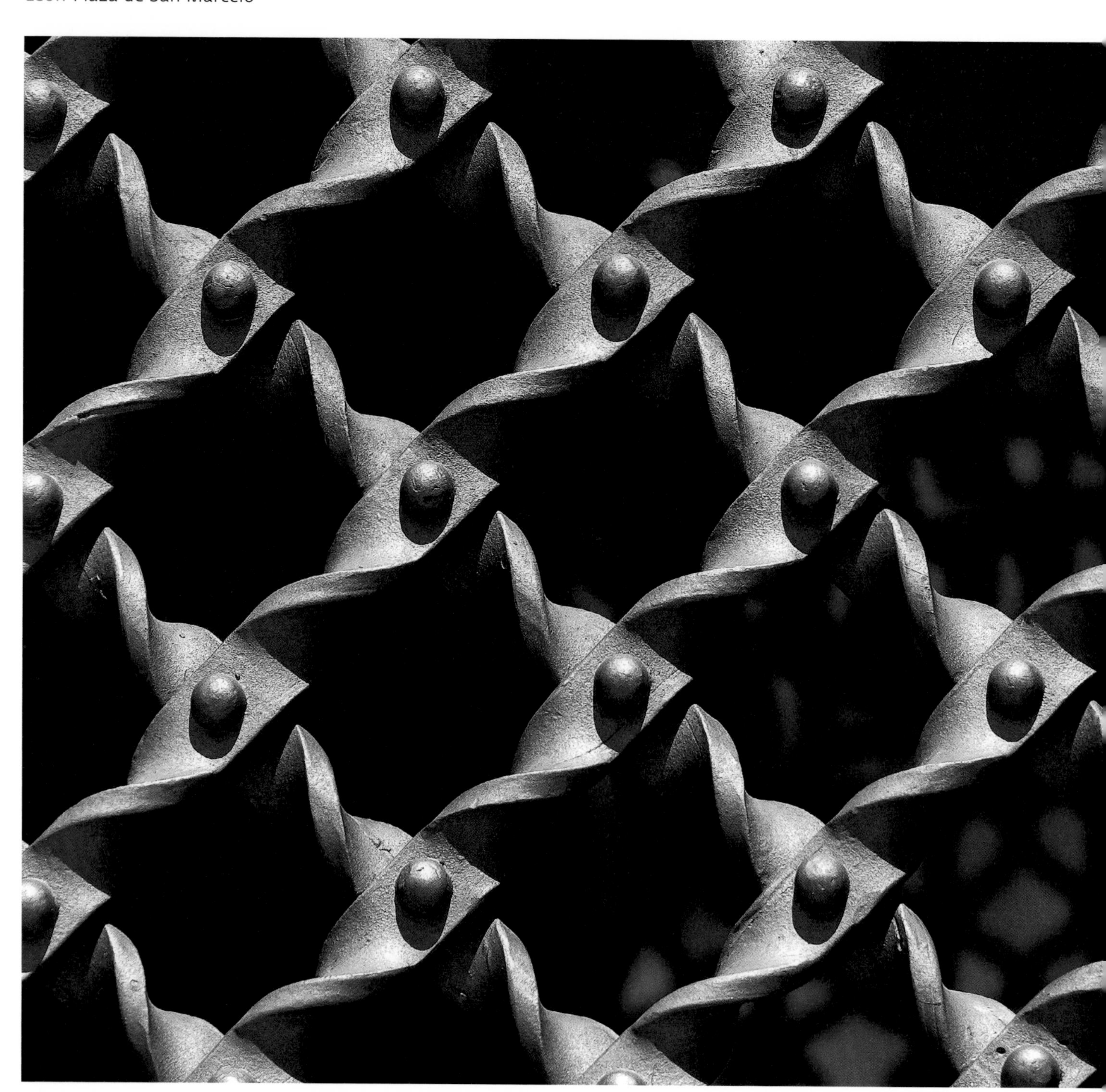

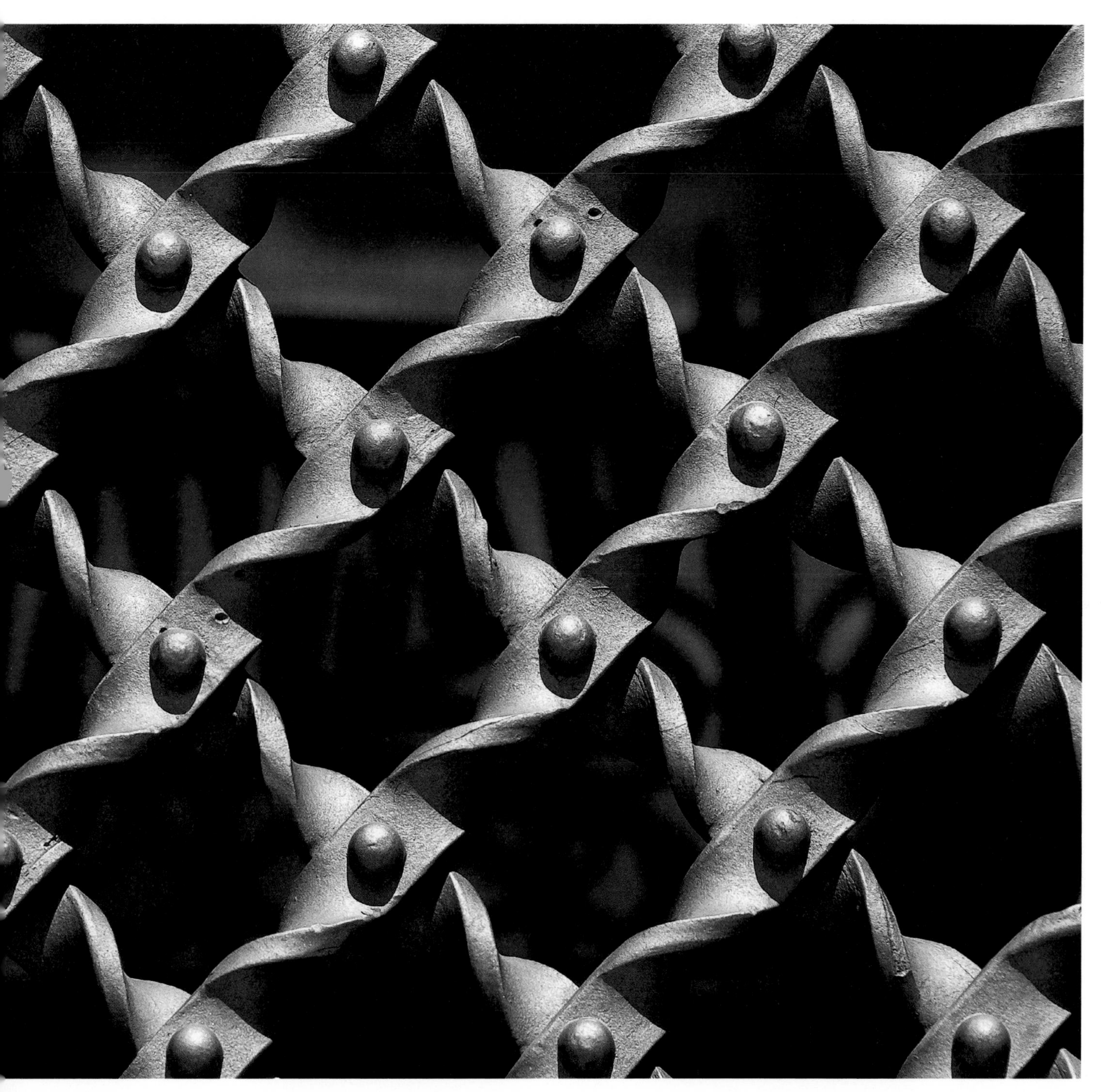

Casa Botines

1891-1892

New headquarters for a traditional company

Juan Homs y Botinás was a Catalan trader who established a textile business in León, popularly known as "Casa Botines". In 1891, his successors, advised by Eusebi Güell, owner of the Barcelona company that supplied them with fabrics, commissioned Gaudí to construct a building of offices, warehouses and flats. The new headquarters changed places, but it took with it the popular name that it still holds today.

The tough weather meant that the work was interrupted during the winter, when the architect devoted his time to preparing the materials for the construction. When the good weather arrived, work began which, thanks to the prior preparation, was completed within a short period of ten months.

For the foundations, Gaudí used the traditional Catalan system of rows of ditches filled with ashlar and concrete instead of the method based on piles, commonly used in local constructions. The use of this technique was widely criticised by local engineers who predicted the collapse of the building. The Casa Botines' lack of integration into the architectural setting of the city of León has often been pointed out. Nevertheless the use of materials such as slate, the Bierzo granite, or the typical pointed form of the towers show the link to local constructions that Gaudí studied in depth using books and photographs.

During the restoration work on the sculpture of St. George in 1950, a lead pipe was found containing documents referring to the building. Specifically, elevation and ground plans were found signed by Gaudí and the owners, along with several issues of local newspapers, a manuscript accrediting ownership of the site and the deed of completion of the works.

Original drawing by Gaudí dated 1891.

The magnificent cast iron lion on the entrance door, symbol of the city and the old medieval kingdom.

Saint George and the dragon, sculpture by Llorenç Matamala over the entrance door.

General view.

Caja España

Casa Botines

1891-1892

A detached residential building with a storeroom and shop, with an almost rectangular ground plan and with a medieval look very similar to that of the neighbouring Episcopal Palace of Astorga.

Erected in the historic centre of León, with the Casa Botines the architect strove to overcome the historical styles, with the aim of presenting a modern concept of architecture and combining the utilitarian, constructive and artistic aspects. There are seven levels with differing uses: the lower-ground floor is the storeroom, the ground floor the shop, the first floor the owners' home, the next two floors for rented accommodation, the attic as a storeroom and a space for the servants' quarters.

The building is structured with load-bearing walls on the floors, whereas in the basement there are iron pillars, only 18 cm thick with which Gaudí obtained a wall-free structure, ideal for commercial transactions.

The outside is notable for the grey granitic stone, which came from the area, arranged in irregular ashlar and discontinuous lines. The four corners are finished with circular towers with which the architect managed to provide the Façades with the visual turn and enable light to enter. The roof is grey slate, a traditional insulator from the snow and rain, and includes six skylights for lighting up the inner courtyards.

The works management, in the absence of Gaudí, was headed by the Catalan constructor Claudi Alsina, who placed the only sculpture in the house over the front door. It is the work of Antoni Cantó and Llorenç Matamala, and was made in Barcelona and represents St. George fighting the dragon. The door is closed with an imposing iron grille, presided over by the image of a lion, the animal that brings to mind the name of the city.

The building was bought in 1931 by the Caja de Ahorros y Monte de Piedad de León, a savings bank, and was later owned by the Caja España, the bank that restored it between 1994 and 1996 and made it their company headquarters.

Heritage Site since 1969. Integral part of the Road to Santiago since 1999.

Initials of Joan Homs, the founder of the company. His successors commissioned this building to Gaudí.

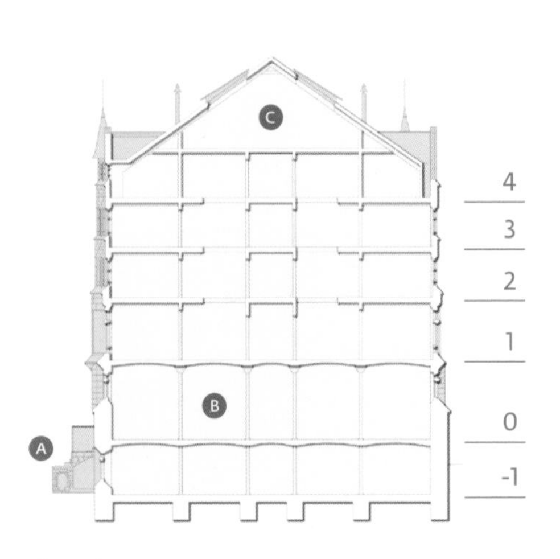

Elevation

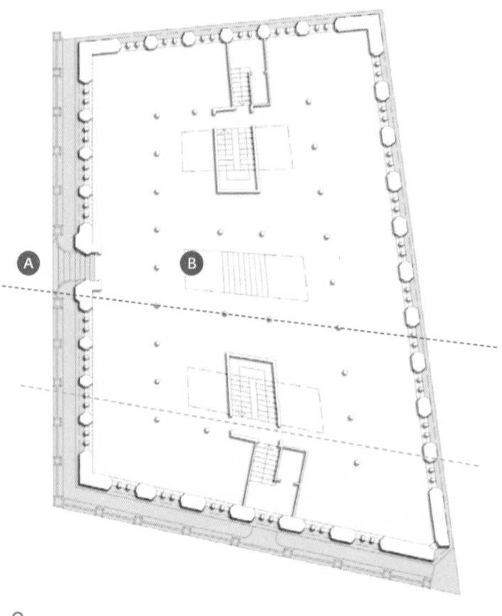

0

Ground floor

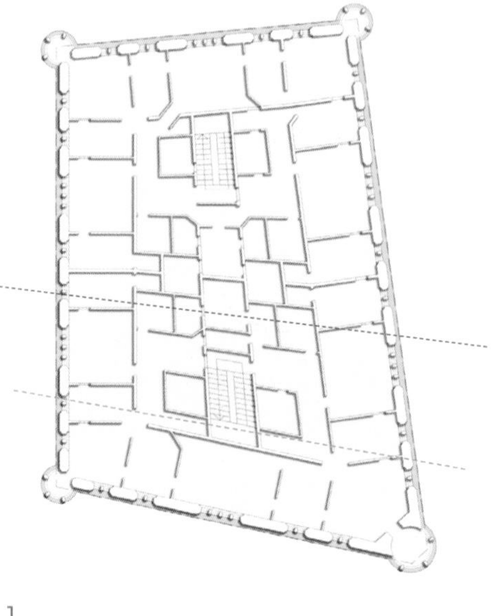

1

First floor

Casa Botines (Casa Fernández y Andrés)
Heirs of Simón Fernández and Mariano Andrés, promoters
December 1891, project
1892, construction
Collaborators:
Claudi Alsina (architect) Nessler Ravirada & Co, Bernard Valero (iron workers)
Joan Coll (carpenter) Antoni Cantó (stonemason) Marià Padró (builder)

Ⓐ Entrance
Ⓑ Shop
Ⓒ Loft

Iron pillars to achieve a space free of walls in the commercial rooms of the ground floor.

Wooden interior of one of the towers situated in the angles of the building.

Cellers Güell
Casa Calvet
Torre Bellesguard
Park Güell
Catedral de Mallorca
Casa Batlló
La Pedrera
Cripta de la Colònia Güell

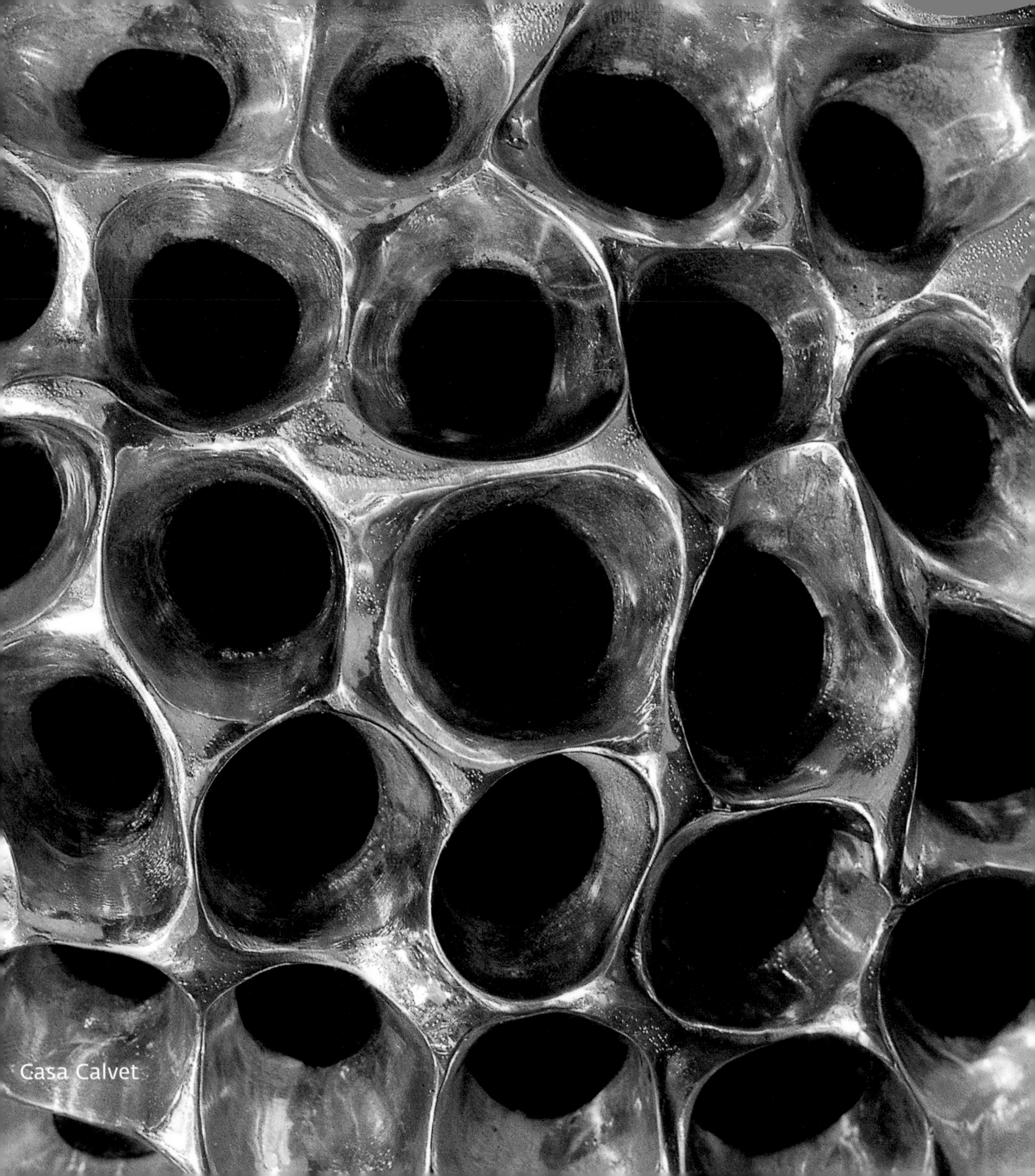

Casa Calvet

Güell Bodegas

Cellers Güell

Garraf (Sitges) Carretera Barcelona-Sitges, km 25

4

Cellers Güell

1895-1901

Facing the Mediterranean

The original project of this piece of work is signed by Gaudí and Güell and dated the 18th of January 1895. However, the authorship of this bodega has often been attributed to Francesc Berenguer i Mestres, collaborator and close friend of Gaudí, who was heavily involved in its construction. Berenguer was well known as a draughtsman and built works such as the sanctuary of Sant Josep de la Muntanya or Gaudí's home in Park Güell. After his death in 1914, Gaudí stated that he had lost his right hand, confirmation of the important role that Berenguer played for the architect.

Eusebi Güell, owner of an area of vineyards in the Garraf region, had these cellars built to bottle the wine he exported to Cuba on the ships of the Compañía Transatlántica.

The Garraf area was a particularly meaningful spot for Güell, who, on the 4th of August 1892, in the main hall of the Güell Palace, performed the first of five acts of a poem entitled Garraf. The poem, written by Ramon Picó i Campanar and given its musical accompaniment by Josep Garcia i Robles, told of the adventures of a character called Garraf, father of three daughters with names of places from the area – Vallbona, Ginesta and Falconera – conceived with the "water woman", a personification of the underground spring hidden beneath the rocks. In fact, one of the count's most ambitious and unrealisable projects consisted of diverting the underground springs of the area in order to supply water to Barcelona.

In 1892 Gaudí sketched a project for a hunting lodge in the Garraf area that was never built.

The Güell Bodegas served their function for quite a few years, later changing owner and today housing a restaurant.

Postcard published in 1910.

Gaudí was always concerned about enhancing the humble elements of the buildings as can be seen in the pinnacle and the chimney.

The shape of the entrance grille recalls the bow of a boat in allusion to the wines that Eusebi Güell exported.

General view.

Cellers Güell

1895-1901

The Güell Bodegas are made up of two buildings: the reception area and the aptly named cava, or cellar. It has a rectangular ground plan and the elevation reveals a pyramidal section that stands out for the way in which the walls are transformed into the roof. It has three levels: the ground floor, used as the depot and bodega; the first floor, for the owner's home and the second floor, for a chapel and viewpoint with views over the Garraf massif and the Mediterranean sea. What stands out here is the abundant use of the parabolic arch and of those deliberately designed elements, such as a small and slender bell tower, chimneys with naturalist finishes and the inclusion of the letter G of the owner carved into the stone on the Façade. The property is built from local stone, in harmony with the rocky landscape of the setting.

The reception area is a building of discrete proportions, made in stone and brick, giving an interesting view over the main door. This is closed off by an iron grille that includes a mesh of the same material, reminding one of the fishermen's nets.

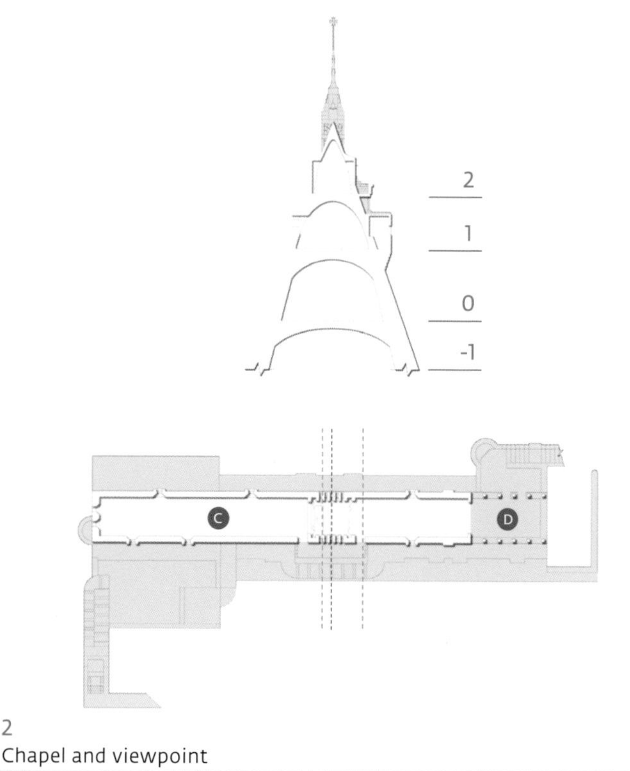

2
Chapel and viewpoint

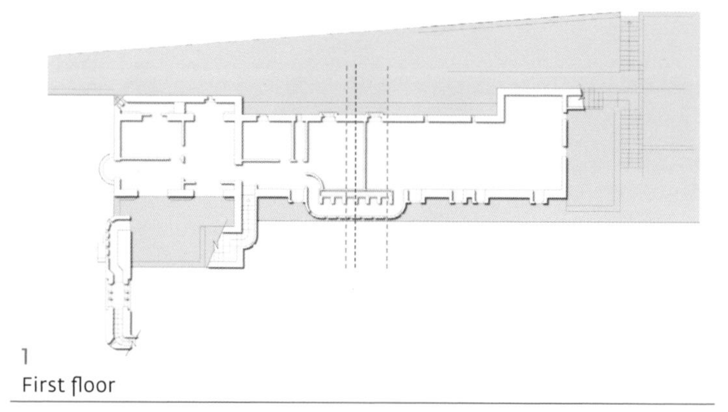

1
First floor

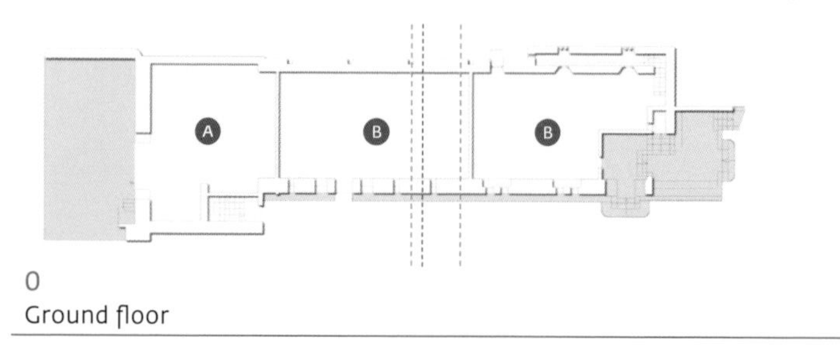

0
Ground floor

Interior of the chapel.

Güell Bodegas
Eusebi Güell i Bacigalupi, promotor
18th of January 1895, project
1895-1901, construction
Francesc Berenguer, collaborating architect

- A Coach house
- B Cellar
- C Chapel
- D Viewpoint

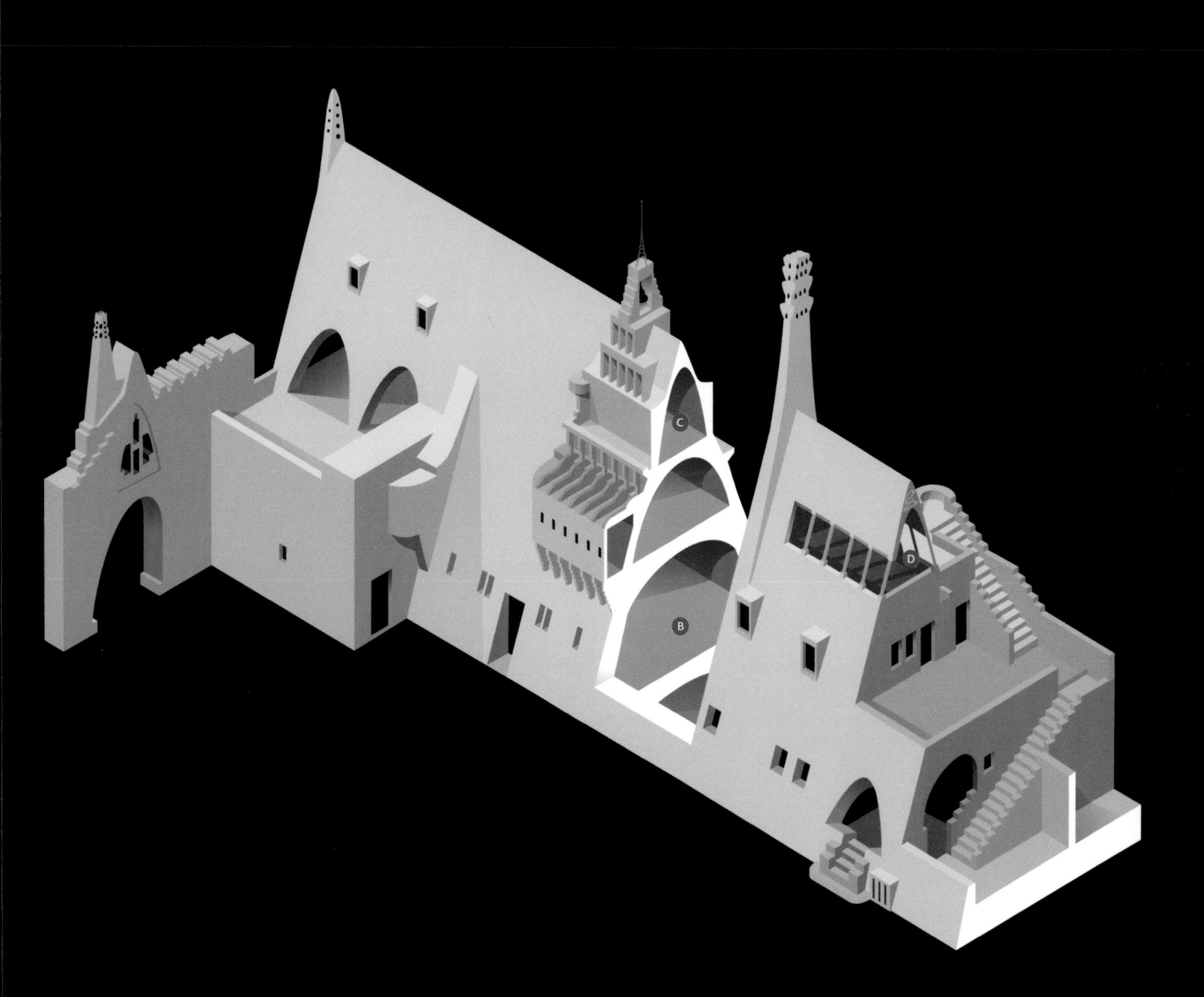

Pavilion of the porter's lodge. Here the masonry work in grey stone from the Garraf used in the cellars combines with the brickwork.

Porch and viewpoint at the entrance of the chapel with catenary arch
and vault.

Casa Calvet

Barcelona Carrer de Casp, 48

Casa Calvet

1898-1900

The Baroque house

Casa Calvet is a residential building built for the Hijos de Pere Màrtir Calvet textile company. It is a transitional piece of work, which although maintaining certain nineteenth-century traits, announces the modernity of the design that the architect would develop in his later works. The small cast iron balconies at the top of the Façade, the furniture, the functional elements such as the peepholes – which Gaudí himself moulded by repeatedly sinking his fingers into the clay – the Marian inscriptions over the Catalan flag of the vestibule of the motto of the Jocs Florals, a poetry festival where flowers are awarded as prizes, "Faith, Homeland and Love", are premonitions of the themes and forms of the Casa Batlló, Park Güell and La Pedrera.

Just as Gaudí himself asserted, the building is inspired by Catalan Baroque, although to the formal exuberance of this style is added the organic and naturalist spirit so typical of Gaudí's work in his later stages. The capitals in the form of palm leaves transform the Solomonic columns of the vestibule into trees, something that also occurs in the Sagrada Família. The doorknocker is an insect over which a cross hits it on knocking, and the furniture has, for the first time, a certain living quality due to its exceptional ergonomic design.

The iconography of the house is a kind of set in homage to Pere Calvet and the shape of a large part of the decoration seems to be inspired by the letter "C". On the main Façade, the columns of the entrance door are textile spools, the industrial enterprise of the Calvet family. Over the threshold of the door, surrounding a cypress tree, a symbol of welcome, appears the owners' initial. The balconies are decorated with forms of the latticed stinkhorn toadstool, which show his love of mycology and over the gallery, two horns of plenty and a pigeon feeding its two chicks, symbolising the fortune Calvet left his family, and in the upper part of the building are the busts of Saint Peter the Martyr, Saint Genesius the Notary and Saint Genesius the Actor, the patron saints of Pere Calvet and of Vilassar de Mar, his birthplace.

Crowned by two crosses, the high part of the building exceeded the height permitted by local by-laws. Gaudí presented a plan in which the excess part appeared marked with a line and he threatened to eliminate it, something that, luckily, was not necessary. The appearance of the main Façade contrasts strongly with the free and modern language of the back Façade. On this he projected large balconies that he embellished with graphite decoration in an assortment of colours that reproduced garlands of flowers around medallions bearing the inscription pmc, Pere Màrtir Calvet.

Postcard from 1905.

Columns of the entrance in the form of textile reels.

Insect of the doorknocker that is crushed by a Greek cross when knocking at the door.

Main façade.

Chocolates Brescó
centro auditivo integral
macso

Casa Calvet
1898-1900

A commercial and residential building between party walls built on one of the then-considered select streets of the new Eixample district of Barcelona. The building is structured on six levels (basement, ground floor, first floor and three more floors) with which it maintains the style of its contemporary buildings. The basement and ground floor were for the family business, the first floor the owners' residence and the other floors were for rent.

Concerned about the correct illumination of the interior, Gaudí built a huge stairwell that joined the two wells, thus achieving the illumination of the inside of the floors. The interior is noteworthy for the decoration of the vestibule and the design of the lift, as well as the resolution of different functional elements, such as the knobs, peepholes and handles. Also of note are the manager's office and offices of the owners' textile business, for which Gaudí designed stools, tables and chairs with the shape adapted to the anatomy of the human body.

The basic construction materials were stone, ceramic tiles, iron and wood, all of it being of first class quality.

In 1900, the Casa Calvet won the prize of the best building in the city, awarded by Barcelona City Council. It was the only building entered into the competition and the prize was given for its excellent hygienic conditions.

The Casa Calvet is still a private residence and for several years now the ground floor has housed a restaurant that has conserved many of the original elements designed by the architect.

National Heritage Site since 1969.

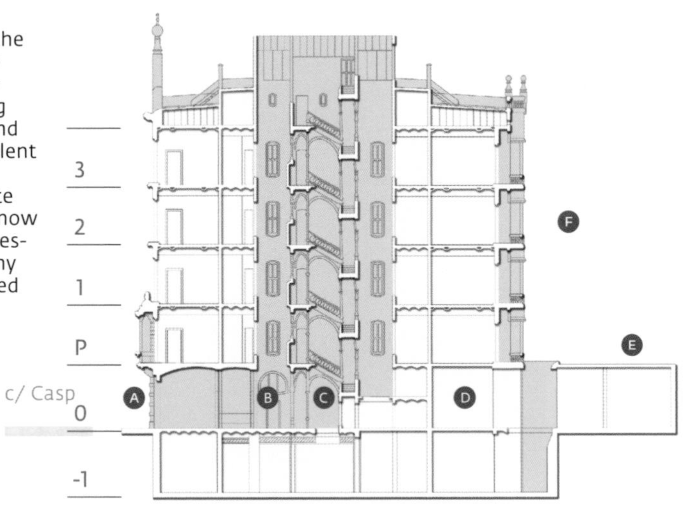

Elevation

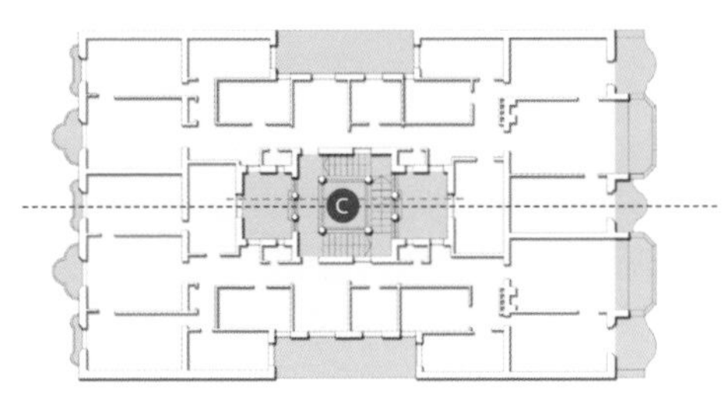

P
Main floor

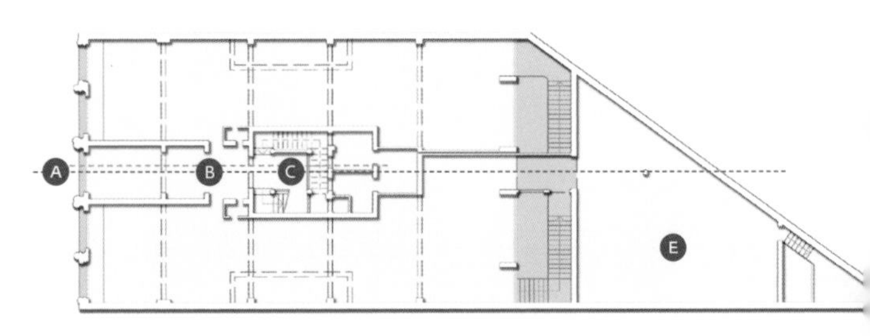

0
Ground floor

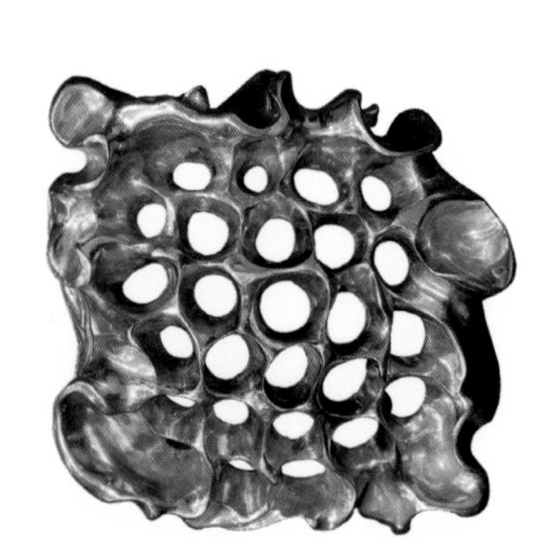

Gaudí achieved the form of the peephole, which recalls a honeycomb, sinking his fingers into the clay.

The furnishing, in oak wood without nails or screws, was also designed by Gaudí.

Casa Calvet
Heirs of Pere Màrtir Calvet, promoter
1898, project | 1898-1900, construction
Collaborators:
Francesc Berenguer, Joan Rubió, Juli Batllevel (architects)
Joan Oños, Lluís Badia, (iron workers) Casas & Bardès (cabinetmakers)
Salvador Boada (marble mason)

- A Entrance
- B Vestibule
- C Lift
- D Offices
- E Courtyard
- F Rear façade

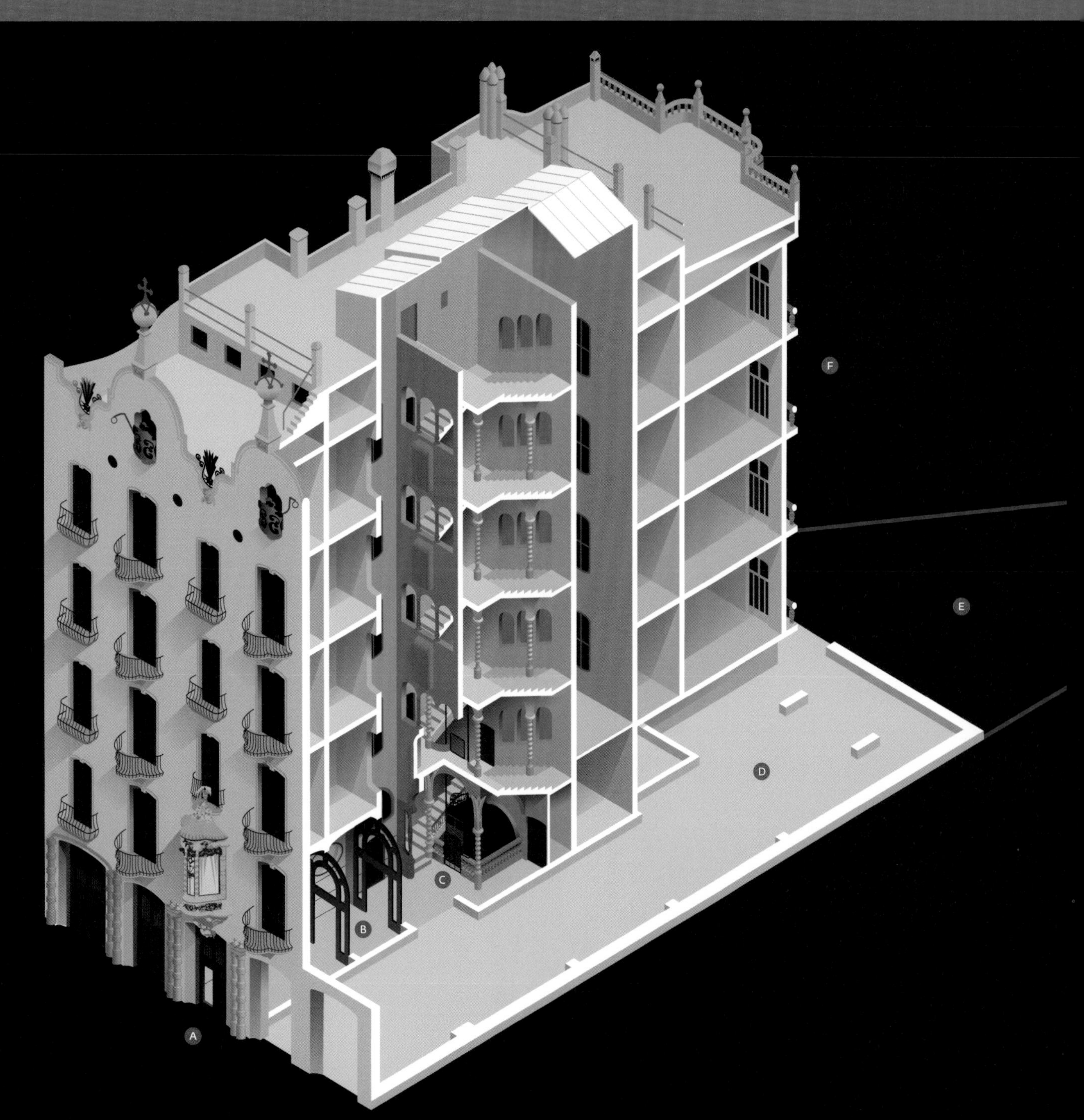

On the crowning of the building are the busts of two patron saints of Vilassar (birthplace of Mr Calvet), of Saint Peter Martyr and two wrought iron works, preceding those of La Pedrera.

Below the gallery, Gaudí placed a C, the initial of Calvet, over the coat of arms of Catalonia and crossed by a cypress tree, symbol of eternal life.

Landing on the first floor where the columns and arches are also inspired by Catalan Baroque.

Over the arch of the lobby a Catalan flag bears an inscription in Catalan that says "Hail the Virgin Mary without conceived sin" and the initials of the Holy Family: Jesus, Mary and Joseph.

Bellesguard Tower

Torre Bellesguard

Casa Figueras

Barcelona Carrer de Bellesguard, 16-20

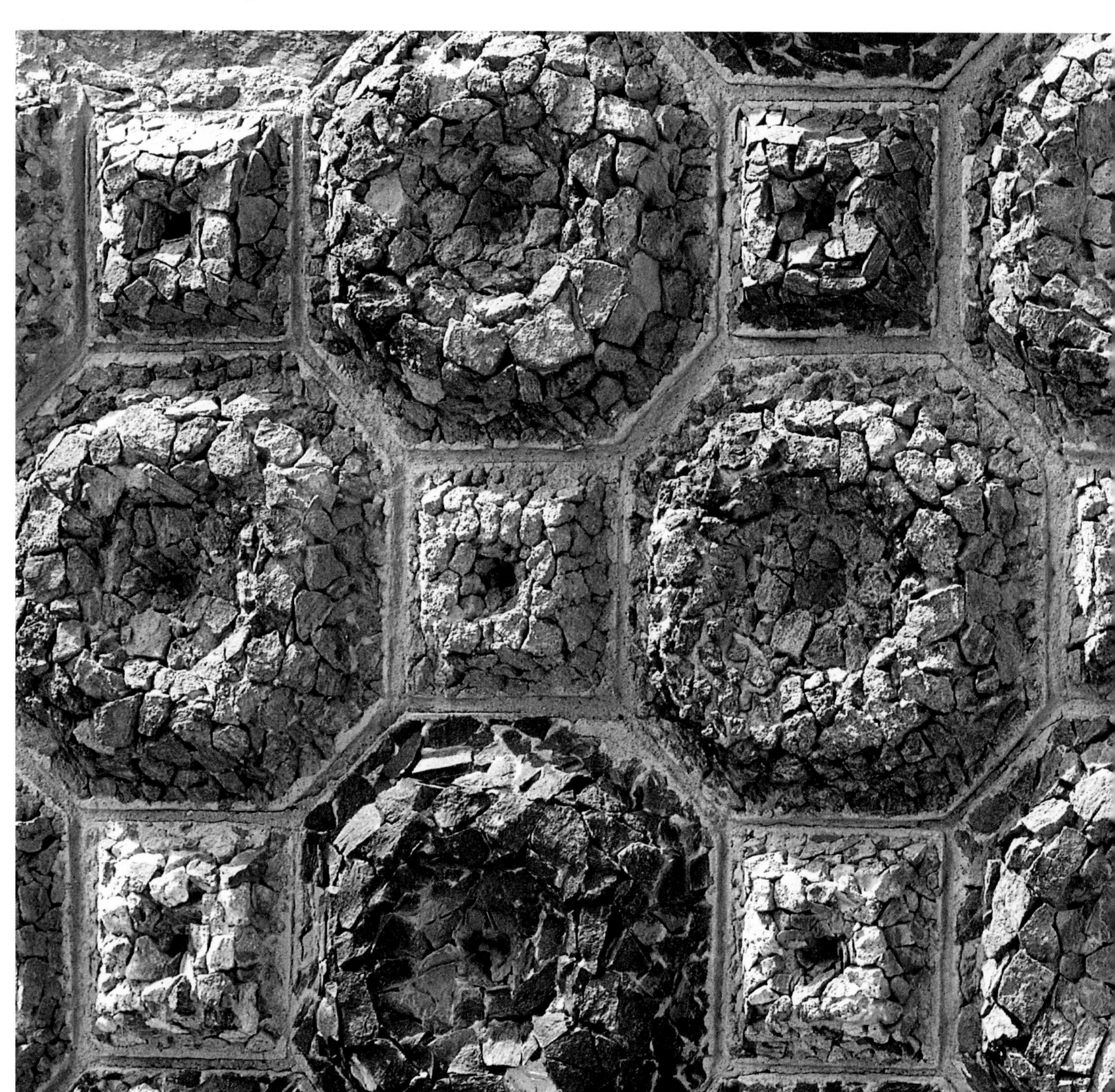

5

Torre Bellesguard

1900-1909

A tower with history

In 1409, one of the popes resulting from the western split in the Church, Benedict XIII, presided over the marriage of Martí I, the last king of the Aragonese Crown, to Margarida de Prades. The bucolic setting of the wedding was a summer palace that the monarch possessed at the foot of the Collserola range and which, due to the splendid views across Barcelona and the sea, was baptised by the poet Bernat Metge with the name of Bellesguard, "Beautiful View".

Four centuries later, Joan Grau i Vallespinós, the bishop of Astorga and a friend of Gaudí, became the owner of the land in which archaeological remains of the ancient royal palace were located. In his will, Grau expressed the desire for the land to be sold and the proceeds to go into building a school for poor children in Reus. In 1900, Maria Sagués bought the estate with Gaudí acting as an intermediary, and to whom she commissioned the construction of a house. Being aware of the symbolic value of the land, he paid his own particular homage to the history of Catalonia, recovering Catalan Gothic to which he added his own personal vision of architecture.

The watchtower, finished with a ceramic mosaic in the colours of the Catalan flag, a royal crown and a four-armed cross, the crenelated walkway enabling the whole roof to be circumvented, the shape of the windows, the lengthened mullioned windows and arches, of a particular Gothic style, give Bellesguard a certain air of a medieval fortress. The rough exterior slate facing contrasts with the clarity and light of the interior which features beautiful white columns with bulbous capitals.

To join Bellesguard with the remains of a tower, between 1903 and 1905, Gaudí re-routed an old path that went past the property and supported it over vaulting sustained by inclining pillars, creating viaducts similar to those of Park Güell. From 1909 onwards, Gaudí stopped working on the site and left it to his collaborator, Domènec Sugrañes, to finish the entrance benches – decorated with fish carrying the Catalan flag and crown in reference to the hegemony between Catalonia and the Mediterranean –, as well as the gardens, the porter's lodge and the decoration on the main stairway, with its spectacular window, interpreted as Venus, the twilight star, in reference to the last king of the Catalan-Aragonese dynasty.

Postcard dated 1905.

The 13th century poet Bernat Metge baptised this place with the name Bellesguard, "beautiful view".

Doorknocker in naturalist forms.

Ornament in cast iron of the handrails.

Torre Bellesguard
1900-1909

The fish on the benches have the four bars and the crown in reference to Catalan hegemony in the Mediterranean during the Middle Ages.

A detached, isolated house, with a square ground plan and 19.5 metres in height and built as a private residence. The exterior is noted for its marked cubic volume and slender angular tower.

It is structured in five levels (lower ground floor, ground floor, first floor and two lofts, the second in the form of an attic) and the inside possesses a very rich atmosphere where highly original constructive and structural solutions are applied. In this sense the stairwell of the house really stands out, the veritable backbone of the building, painted white and illuminated by a stained-glass window of intense colours that stick out towards the exterior in the form of a star.

The roofing is also notable, structurally resolved with the two levels of lofts, one as a support and the other as a coronation, built with walls, partitions and solid open brickwork arches which lighten the weight on this high part of the house. The crowning level forms the external appearance of the roof, flanked by merlons and a walkway.

The building is made in solid brick which Gaudí covered with local slate classified according to the grey, brown, yellow and green shades, recreating the Roman technique of Opus incertum, thus maintaining a dialogue with the natural setting.

The architect used a curious system to produce the speckled masonry of the Façade. He started with a clay model to obtain a plaster mould, at the bottom of which he placed small stones which, on being covered with the mortar, stuck to it, thereby creating an original surface in the final piece.

National Heritage Site since 1969.

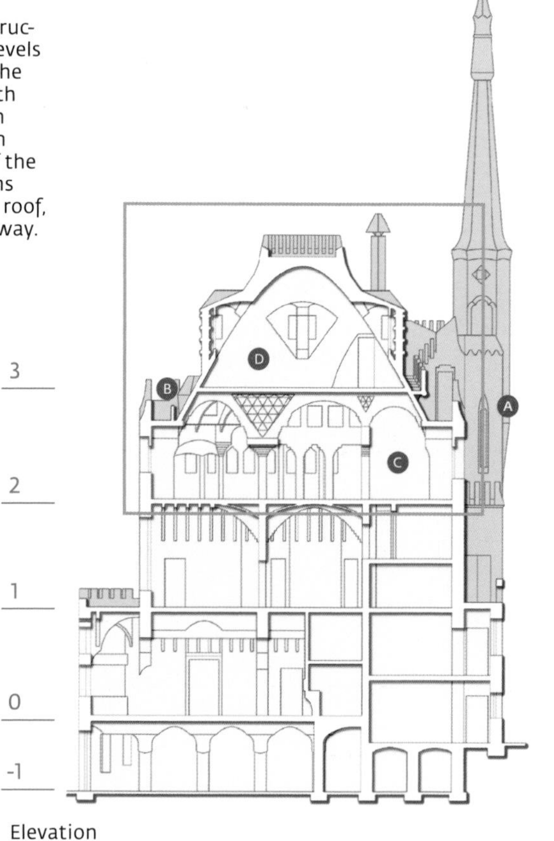

Elevation

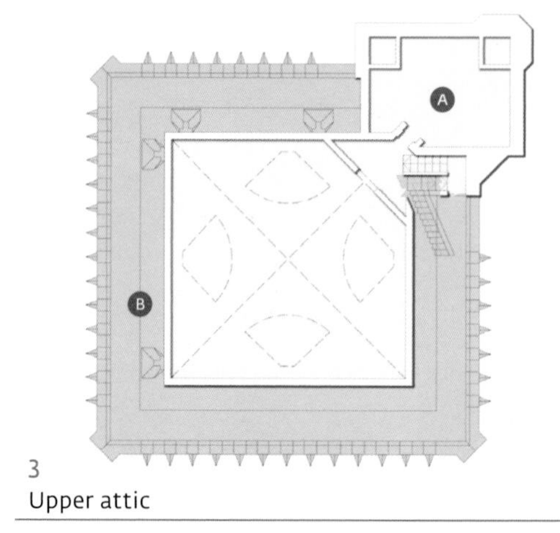

3
Upper attic

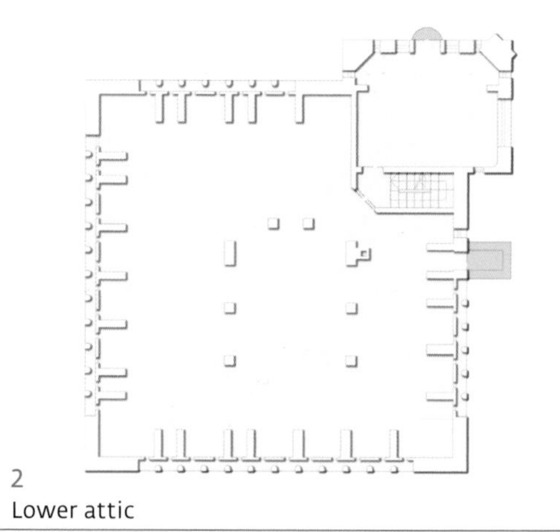

2
Lower attic

Bellesguard Tower (Casa Figueras)
Maria Sagués i Molins, promoter
1900, project
1900-1909, construction
Domènec Sugrañes i Gras, collaborating architect

A) Tower
B) Walkway
C) Lower attic
D) Upper attic

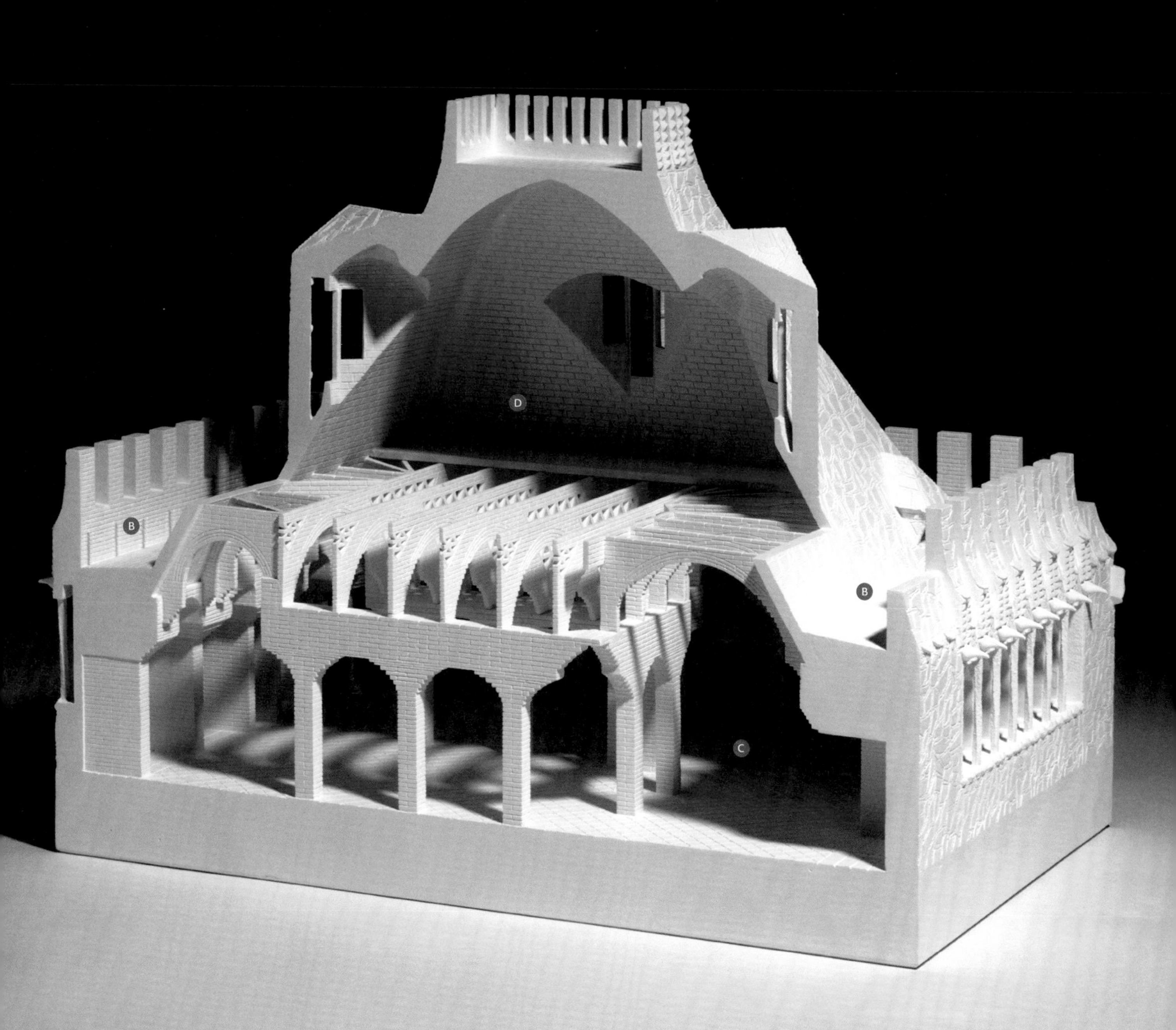

The spectacular stained glass of the main stairway is interpreted as Venus, the star of the sunset, as well as the dawn.

The well-lit lobby of friendly and rounded forms contrasts with the external appearance similar to that of a medieval fortress.

Trefoil arches in parabolic form of the first loft, where Gaudí fused functionality and aesthetics.

Walkway on the flat roof of the attic.

Gaudí rerouted a path that went through the inside of the estate to integrate the remains of the medieval palace in Bellesguard. To support this path, he designed a viaduct with leaning pillars similar to those of Park Güell.

Park Güell

Barcelona Carrer d'Olot, s/n

6

13

Park Güell

1900-1914

The Utopian Arcade

At the end of the 19th century, landscape gardens spread across Europe. They were spaces where all kinds of social events could be held and evoked distant times and places as diverse as the classical temples, Gothic ruins or prehistoric caves.

Park Güell was conceived as a private urban development for the elite of Barcelona. It should have been a self-sufficient space in which all the residents would have the necessary services: private chapel, market, theatres, water reserves, etc. Güell and Gaudí wanted this community to be able to maintain itself distanced from a city ravaged with epidemics and social conflicts. They did not want the tramway to reach there and they surrounded the property with a wall that protected and isolated this bucolic retreat.

Between 1900 and 1907 the urban development project was unfolded, governed by a series of very strict construction rules. Half of the land was earmarked as green area and the rest parcelled off into triangular sites with a surface area of between 1,000 and 2,000 square metres. The conditions stipulated for each site were very demanding indeed. Only a part could be built on and the rest had to be for a private garden. The height and location of the houses was also limited so that the sunlight and sea views would not be blocked out in any way. The park wall, decorated with medallions on which the words Park Güell can be read, envelops each of the porters' lodges that flank the main entrance like a ribbon. The colouring of the ceramic tiles, the sinuous profile, the tower crowned by a four-armed cross or the chimney in the form of a mushroom are just some of the features of these buildings, stylistically related to the Casa Batlló.

The lodge on the left-hand side, which was originally a reception with a telephone, is today the bookshop, and the one on the right, formerly the home of the porters, is now the park's Information and Activity Centre.

To some writers, the park provides an allusion to the sacred city of Delphos. In Park Güell the agora, temple and theatre of the Greek Polis are transformed into a unique architectural monument made up of the stairway, the hypostyle hall and the square-cum-theatre. Gaudí himself stated that, "I have made the archaic Doric colonnade of Park Güell just as the Greeks would have done in a Mediterranean colony". The Sacred Way, the initiation path that led to the highest point of the Polis, is also reinterpreted in the park by the path which, passing through the viaducts, rises to the Calvary.

The stairway, which runs among walls covered in *trencadís* mosaic, has three small pools that successively collect water coming from the tank. In the first we come across the salamander – one of the most popular decorative elements of the park – and in the next one, a snake's head rises from the Catalan coat of arms, and in the last, the small rockery garden and aquatic plants form a miniature landscape.

The hypostyle hall, with 86 columns, has the ceiling decorated with large circular panels, produced by Jujol according to Gaudí's instructions. Here, the collage of ceramic and glass *trencadís* reaches its maximum expression. The same technique was used for the ceramic covering of the bench in the square, an important piece of 20th century abstract art. The square, also called the theatre, is designed as a stage that has Barcelona and the sea as the backdrop and was fitted with mobile wooden stands.

The constructions inside the park are perfectly adapted to the irregular lie of the land. One example of the integration of the architecture into the natural environment is the viaducts in the park. They were built from material taken directly from the land itself and their leaning columns seem to be tree trunks sprouting from the ground. Structured into three sections – the lower, central and upper viaduct – they form a climbing route that takes us to the highest point in the park, where Gaudí originally planned a chapel that was never eventually built. In its place he produced a Calvary, the shape of which reminds one of the Talayot burial chambers in the Balearics.

Gaudí went to live in the park in 1906, accompanied by his father and niece. He lived in the showhouse built by Francesc Berenguer and remained there until 1925, when he moved to the workshops of the Sagrada Família.

By 1907, only two plots had been sold and the failure of this utopian urban development was plain to see. In 1923, the Council bought the park from the Güell family and turned it into a public space. In 1963 the Friends of Gaudí association bought the architect's house, which today houses the Gaudí House-Museum.

Postcard from 1907. The claws of the salamander have a fiercer appearance than those of later restorations.

Postcard published in 1908.

The entrance pavilions lead to the flight of steps that rise to the Hypostyle Hall, which in turn supports part of the large square.

Park Güell

1900-1914

A private residential urban development, never originally designed as a park, and planned in accordance with the British taste for "garden cities" (thus taking the English name park inscribed on the main entrance).

Gaudí partially developed the 15 hectares of land in the district of La Salut in Gràcia, in the northern part of the city, in an area known as the Muntanya Pelada (the bald mountain), rather rocky and full of slopes. Gaudí designed all the necessary services for the community, with a project that encompassed seventy sites with gardens, building viaducts, squares and streets, closure walls and porters' lodges, as well as a large entrance stairway and a hypostyle hall for a covered market. Over this is a large public square, bordered by a winding bench built from ergonomically designed prefabricated modules.

The square is a collecting point for rainwater, which is channelled through the columns and taken to a tank below the hypostyle hall, where it is stored to be used for watering.

An outstanding feature of Park Güell is the integration of architecture with nature, the two concepts always in total harmony. In order to save the natural slopes, Gaudí built viaducts from brick pillars, which he covered with stone obtained from the excavations. He also thought about the vegetation, respecting the existing plantlife and planting new species in the park, such as carob trees, palm trees, wisteria and rosemary.

National Monument since 1969. UNESCO World Heritage Site.

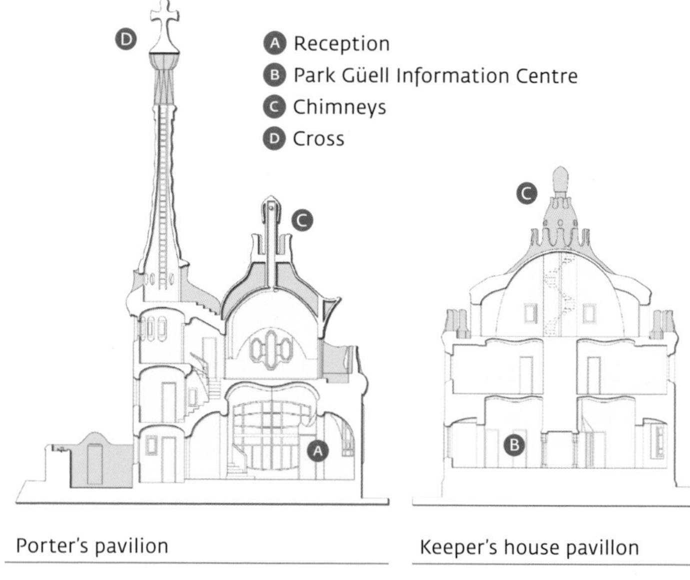

Porter's pavilion

Keeper's house pavillon

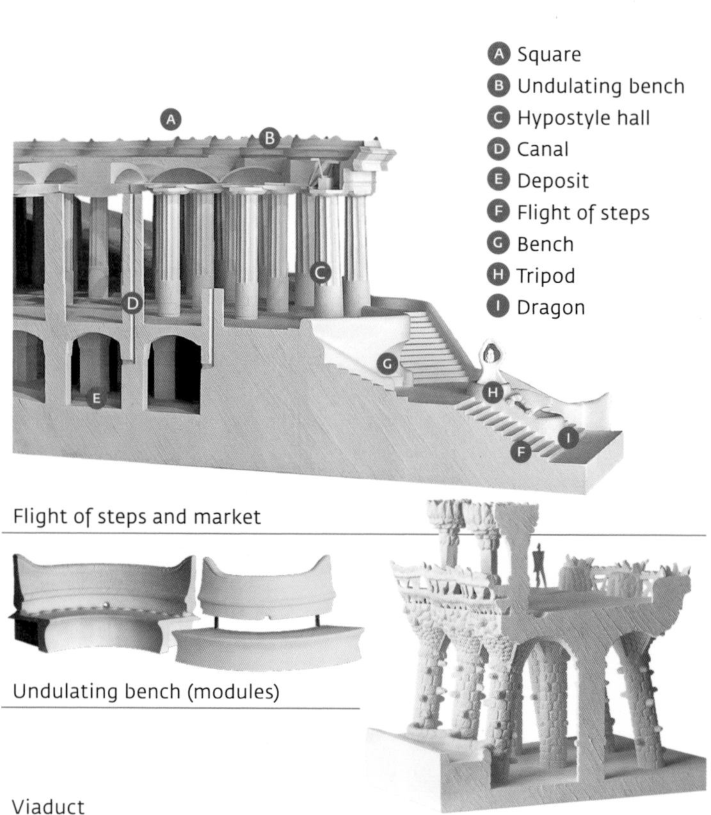

Flight of steps and market

Undulating bench (modules)

Viaduct

Inside of the Gaudí House-Museum.

Park Güell
Eusebi Güell i Bacigalupi, promoter
1900-1912, project | 1900-1914, construction
Collaborators:
Joan Rubió, Francesc Berenguer, Josep Maria Jujol (architects) Peris de Onda, Hijo de Jaime Pujol i Baucis, Sebastià Ribó (ceramists) Llorenç Matamala (sculptor) Ricard Opisso (illustrator) Hermanos Badia (iron workers) Agustí Masip, Josep Pardo, Juliano Bardier (constructors)

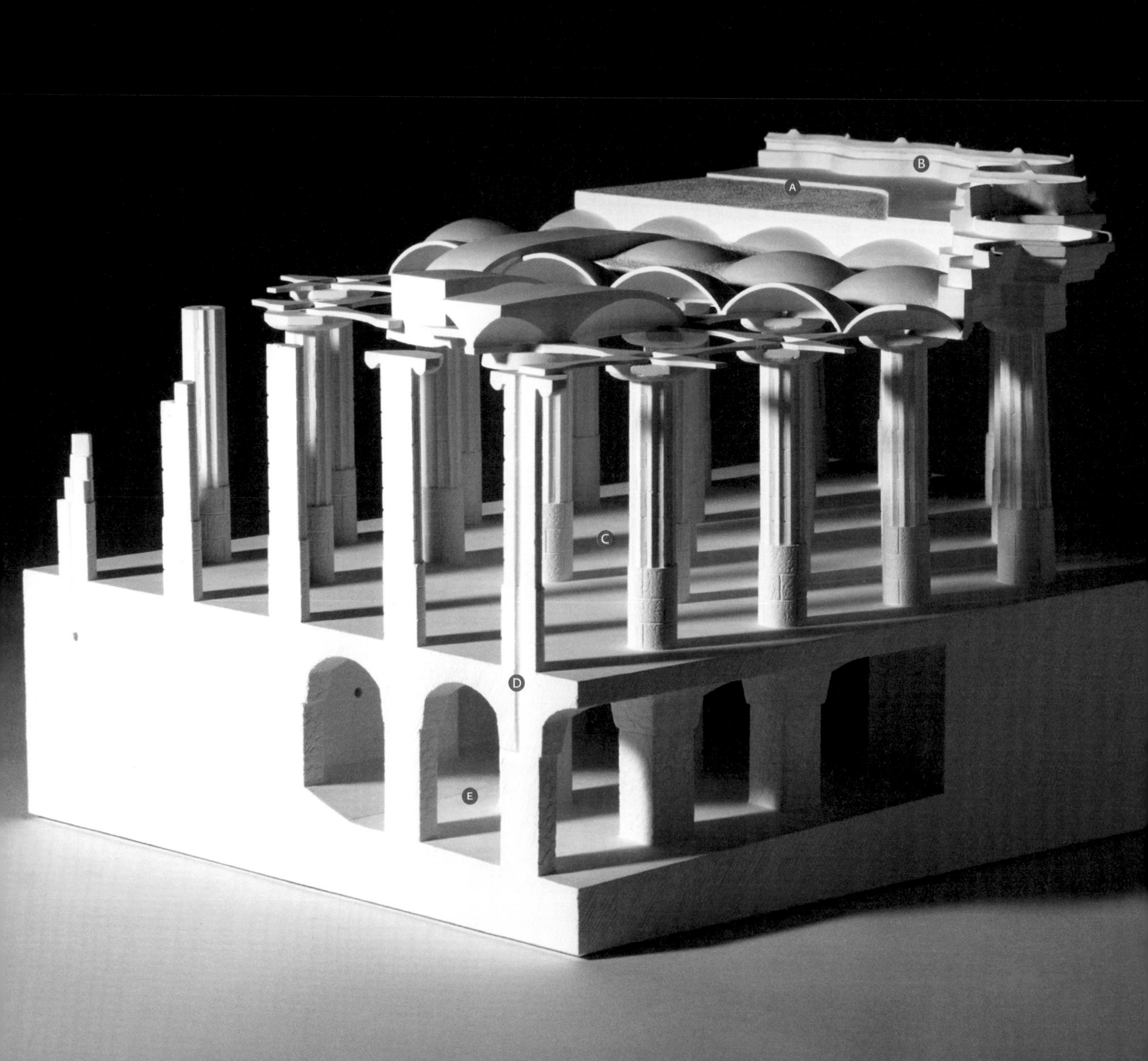

The luminous, imaginative and dreamlike nature of the roofs of the entrance pavilions contrast with the sober, almost atavistic, structure of the three crosses (in the background).

In the last but one section of the flight of steps is the famous fountain of the salamander.

This extraordinary salamander, a legendary animal packed with symbolism, works as the overflow of the deposit placed below the colonnade.

The Hypostyle Hall, a very personal homage by Gaudí to Doric style, was the space planned for the weekly market of the urbanisation.

The curved line and the winding undulation dominate the architectural rhythm of Park Güell, which reaches its maximum expression in the bench of the square, a prodigy of decoration with the *trencadís* technique that produces abstract compositions in line with the early non-figurative paintings of Kandinsky.

In this section of the Washerwoman Porch, Gaudí erases the distinction between columns, ceilings and walls creating a structure that recalls the inside of a wave.

The central column of the carriage shelter of the entrance is in the form of a glass and is inspired by those in some Romanesque crypts.

Show chalet that Francesc Berenguer built and in which Gaudí lived as from 1906. Today it is the Gaudí House-Museum.

Over a structure that recalls the prehistoric talayots of Menorca, Gaudí placed the three crosses of the Calvary. That of Jesus and the Good Thief are crowned by a pyramid and the third is an arrow.

Catedral de Mallorca

Palma de Mallorca Plaça de l'Almoina

Catedral de Mallorca

1903-1914

Restoration

A liturgical restoration

In 1901, Pere Joan Campins commissioned Gaudí to restore the Cathedral of Mallorca. The architect presented a project in which he proposed the following reforms: take down the altar-pieces to free the space of the presbytery and place the choir there, which was in the centre of the nave; place new pulpits, place a baldaquin over the main altar, open the blind Gothic windows, decorate the cathedral with furniture and paintings, and open the chapel to place the tombs of Jaume II and Jaume III of Mallorca. In 1903, the canons gave their approval of the proposed reforms and the architect moved to Mallorca with his collaborators.

One of the most interesting interventions was the replacement of the old stained-glass windows with primary colours which, one behind another and lit up by the sun, produce the secondary colours providing the desired effect by means of varied gradations. These stained-glass windows, designed by Torres i Garcia, are attributed to the leading Barcelona firms of Hijos de E. R. Amigó and Rigalt, Granell y Cía.

The times when Gaudí and his collaborators stayed in Mallorca are accompanied by many anecdotes, among which feature the incident that Jujol provoked on painting the choir stalls. He painted "La sang d'Ell sobre nosaltres" [His blood over us] on them. The canons took it personally and felt insulted and immediately after the death of Bishop Campins, Gaudí's main defender, they made the architect leave the work.

Despite everything, this reform was considered as being a veritable revitalisation of the cathedral, both in terms of recovering spaces and in the renewal of its liturgical meaning. This is shown in a letter dated 1909 by the priest Miquel Costa i Llobera where he wrote, "Gaudí, restoring the See of Mallorca, has revealed the entire meaning of its theological sense".

Postcard from 1913.

Detail of the ceramic decoration on the walls surrounding the choir and the episcopal chair.

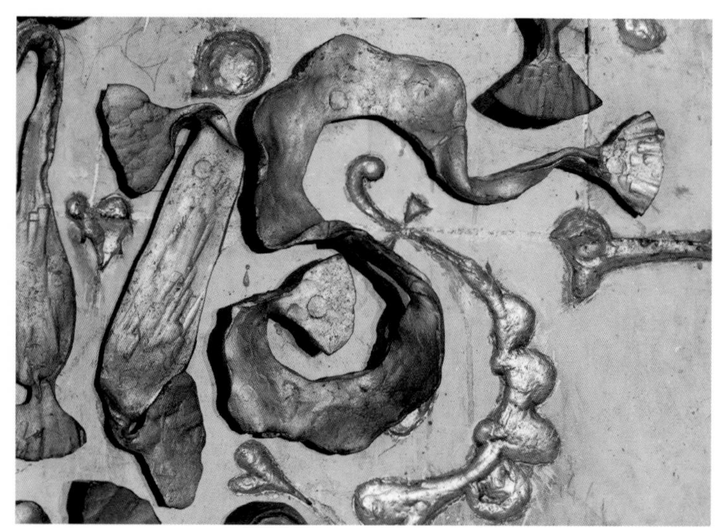

Cast iron letters on the wall of the episcopal chair.

The fantastic baldachin beneath the vaulting.

Paintings over the choir stalls in which Josep Maria Jujol had a leading role.

In the choir, this painting symbolises the Resurrection.

Steps for the exhibition of the Holy Sacrament in the main altar.

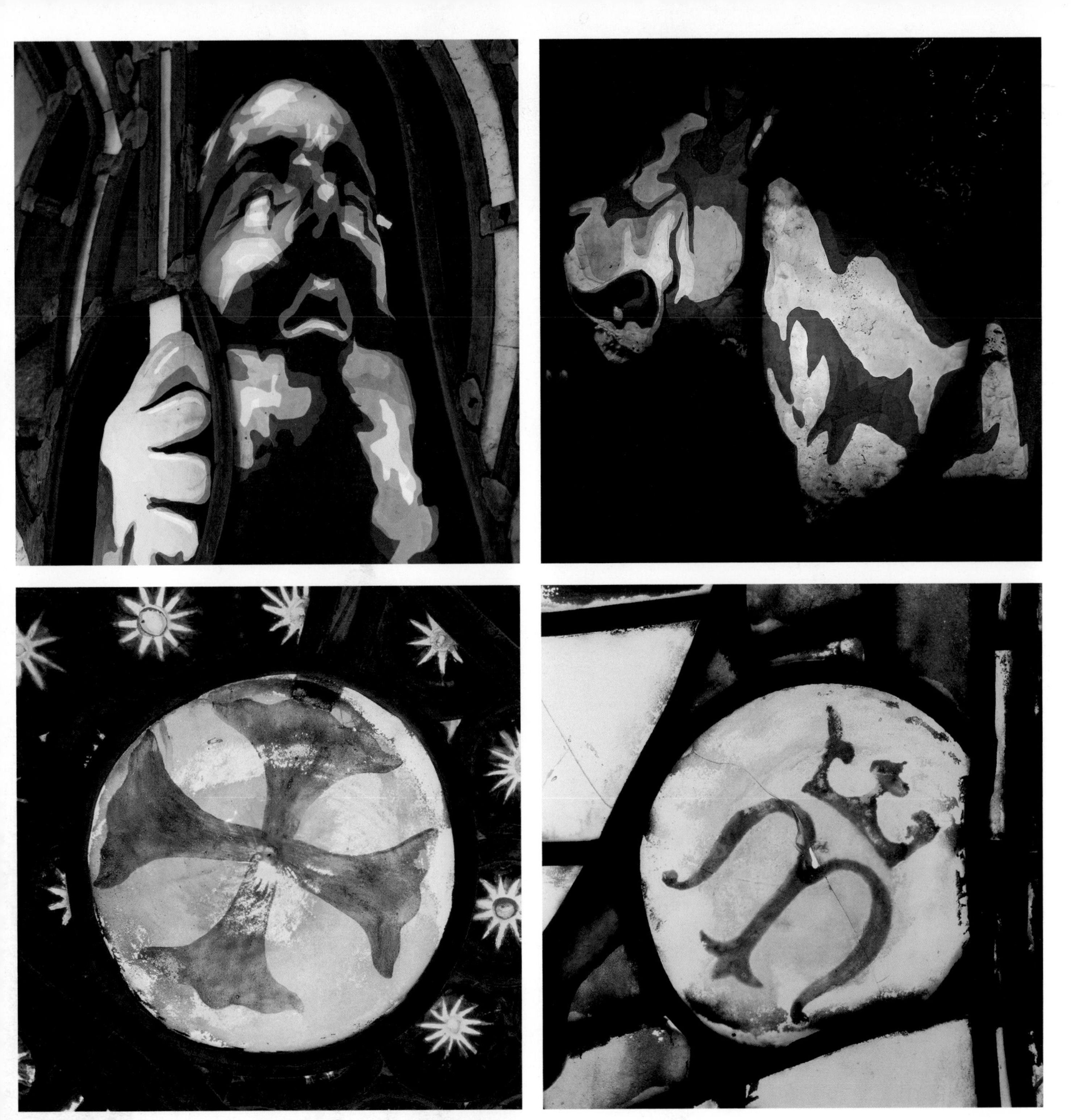

Details of the display cabinets in the chapel of Sant Bernard (above) and of the Episcopal Palace (below).

Casa Batlló

Barcelona Passeig de Gràcia, 43

7

Casa Batlló
1904-1907

Consolidation of a style

Placed beside Casa Amatller (1898), by the architect Puig i Cadafalch, and Casa Lleó Morera (1902), by Domènech i Montaner, Casa Batlló, built later, forms together with the other buildings, the "apple of discord", a block (*manzana* in Spanish means both apple and block) of the Eixample district in which these three important pieces of work converged, showing the diversity in aesthetic orientation of Barcelona's modernist architects.

The maelstrom of urban development at the time and the clients' desire for ostentation had a notable influence in the way that artists, in some form or other, became participants in a competition. Gaudí, aware of this phenomenon, worked with a certain irony and responded to the straight forms of the neighbouring Casa Amatller by creating a sinuous Façade which undulated like an enormous multicolour sail. However, in order not to break completely with the adjoining building, the architect moved the tower with the lettering of the Sagrada Família – originally designed to be in the centre – and designed a moulding where the two houses joined.

Gaudí wanted his pieces of work to be living works and, influenced by the theories of John Ruskin, thought that this was shown through colour and form, qualities that are dazzlingly expressed in the Casa Batlló. For the colour of the Façade facing, the architect used ceramic discs from Mallorca and glass of different shades arranged in *trencadís* mosaic. The outstanding appearance of the polychromy in the Casa Batlló reminds one of the colourist essences of the contemporary artistic movements such as the Fauvism of Matisse, or the water lily series of Claude Monet.

The curved forms, producing the sensations of sinuosity and movement, predominate all over the building and the Façade in particular, which was chiselled away by the workers until it became an undulating surface.

The thin columns of the galleries are tibias from which plantlife begins to sprout, the balconies are bare skulls, the doors to the flats have carved relief forms of bones and the wooden banister on the private stairway is the skeletal form of a gigantic backbone. These kinds of elements are symbols of death, but also of life and regeneration. This fact is highly significant since the Casa Batlló is, in a way, a work of regeneration that is raised over the dead styles of the past. Any reference to historicism had now been finally overcome. The language used was totally modern and its relationship was no longer established with the historicist academicism and nineteenth-century style of the past, but with the new realities of the modern 20th century.

Postcard published in 1907.

Detail of the balconies in which the iron panel seems like the natural volumes of parchment.

Scales of the roof interrupted by the *trencadís*.

The four-armed cross over a bulbous structure stands out in the crowning of the building.

Casa Batlló
1904-1907

Reform and modernisation of a commercial and residential building between party walls. It is one of the most radical interventions made by Gaudí, who did not hesitate in remaking the entire main Façade of the old building, with fluid forms, sinuous undulations and an elaborate vitreous *trencadís* skin that shines with differing intensity according to the position of the sun.

The property is made up of seven floors (basement, ground floor, first floor, four more floors and the attics). On the first floor, also called the main floor and built as the owner's home, he projected an enormous gallery with highly expressive osseous and naturalist forms, in which he included a large sash window with an ingenious system that enabled it to be opened fully to the outside. The home is entered by a sumptuous, independent stairway, closed off from the other residents. It is worth noting the special attention given to the Batlló family home, for which Gaudí invented devices that would provide more inner light and ventilation, built the famous curved and unending ceilings and walls and designed the private chapel of the house and all the furniture, from the doors to the tables, chairs and stools.

Gaudí also modified the inner courtyards of the old building and widened them with the aim of letting air and light pass through, which is filtered down to the ground floor by a large central skylight. The gradation of colour in the inner courtyard goes from deep blue at the top down to white at the bottom, and the size of the windows, which get larger in the lower floors, are the result of Gaudí's desire to control the entry of light into the building.

Gaudí also reformed the rear Façade, on which he placed large balconies and once again embellished with *trencadís*, covered with differently coloured ceramic scales, to which he added a bulbous-shaped tower culminating in a four-armed cross, decorated with the anagrams of the Sagrada Família.

The Casa Batlló is still a private property and is partially open for the public to visit. National Heritage Site since 1969. UNESCO World Heritage Site.

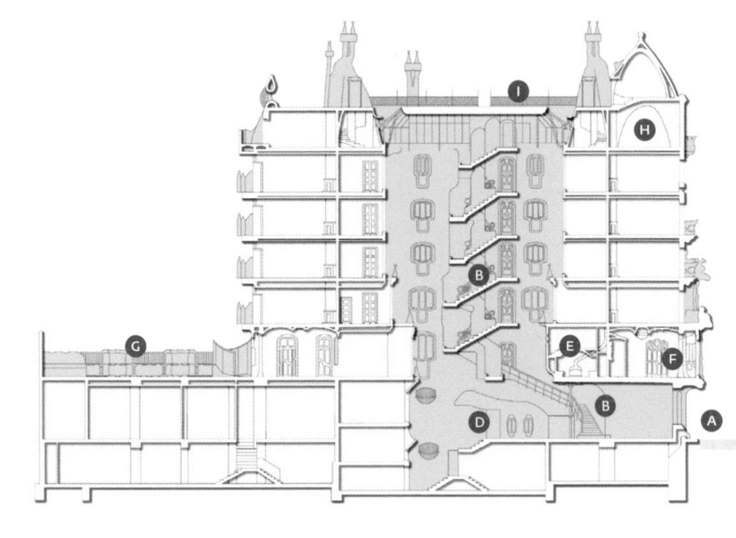

Section

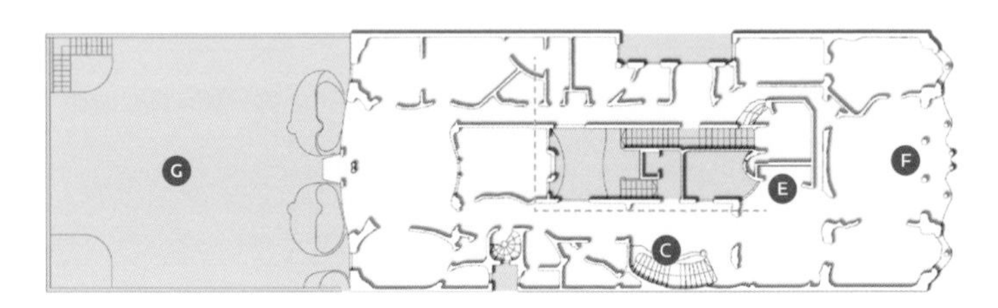

1
Main floor

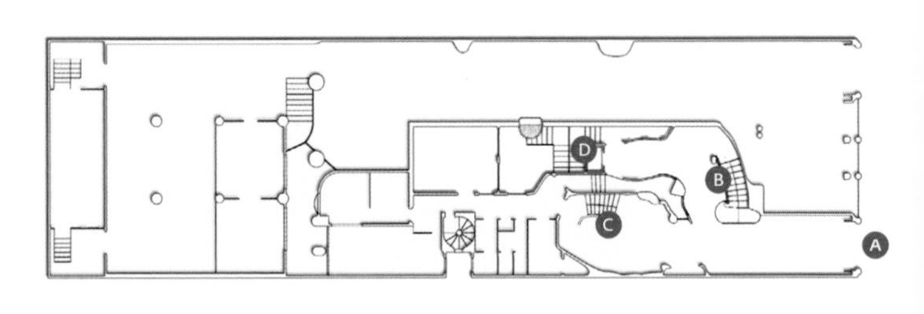

0
Ground floor

Although Gaudí designed this pavement of hexagonal slabs with motifs of marine fauna for Casa Batlló, it was installed in La Pedrera. Today it decorates the pavements of Passeig de Gràcia.

Casa Batlló
Josep Batlló i Casanovas, promotor
26th of October 1904, project | 1904-1907, construction
Collaborators:
Doménec Sugrañes, Joan Rubió (architects) Josep Limona, Joan Matamala, Carles Mani (sculptors) Hermanos Badia (iron workers) Casas & Bardès (cabinetmakers) Pujol Baucis, Sebastià Ribó (ceramists) Pelegrí Workshops (glaziers) Joan Bertran (model maker) Josep Canaleta, Josep Bayó (constructors)

- A Entrance
- B Resident's stairway
- C First floor stairway
- D Lift
- E Fire place
- F Gallery
- G Rear courtyard
- H Loft
- I Flat roof

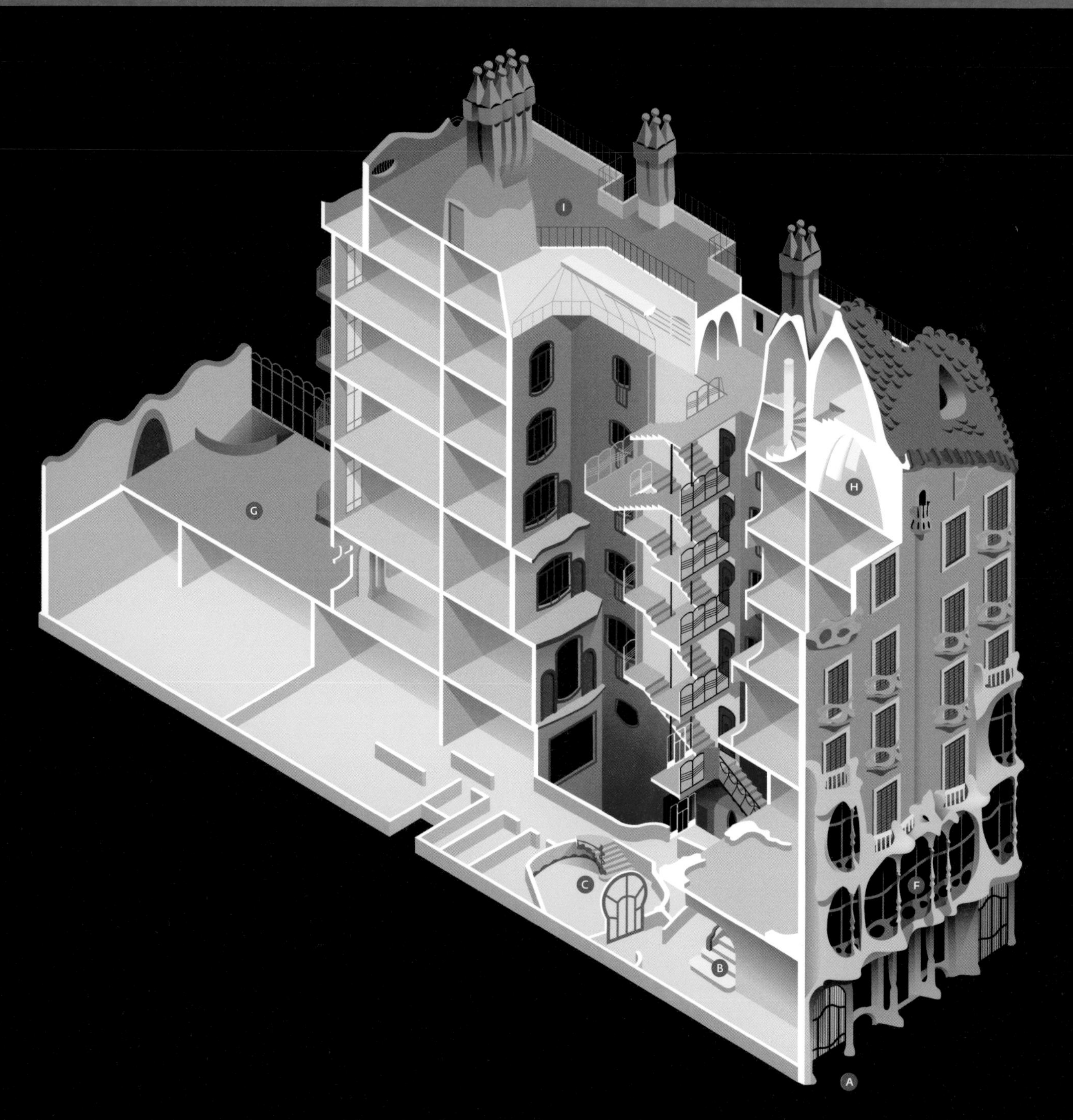

Ceramic discs over *trencadís* on the main façade in a composition that refers to pictorial impressionism.

The railings of the façade balconies, in cast iron moulded into "soft" forms, recall carnival masks over which the confetti of the façade rains.

The columns of the galleries in the form of tibias from which the vegetation sprouts emphasise the organicist nature of the building.

The main room, in which the curved lines give the sensation of space in movement, opens out to the street via stained glass windows decorated with *sibas*, the coloured glass paste discs.

The private stairway that leads to the first floor is of oak wood and the carved pieces of the ornamental top of the steps follow one another like the vertebrae of a dragon's backbone inside a cave.

The walls of the lobby, stuccoed in a light pearl grey, do not have arrises and continue to form the ceiling of soft curves. The beginning of the handrail of the stairs forms an undulation that recalls the movement of a whip.

In the well, and in relation to the light they can capture, the windows are larger in the lower floors and decrease in size as they approach the skylight.

Gaudí decorated the well brilliantly with ceramic tiles of flat pieces and others in relief in a chromatic degradation that goes from cobalt blue next to the skylight, where the light enters with more intensity, to white at the bottom, going through blue, sky blue and pearl grey.

The chimney, embedded into the wall and with seating in the style of the traditional Catalan farmhouses, exemplifies the fusion between beauty and functionality, the essence of design.

The ceiling of the central room is level and forms a whirlpool, a reference to water as well as the idea of generation in nature, a common concept in Gaudí.

The loft is built by means of partitioned vaults of a parabolic outline, plastered and painted in white. A place used for everyday tasks (storage, washroom and drying area) enriched by the intervention of Gaudí, a constant factor in his treatment of the modest or marginal spaces of the buildings.

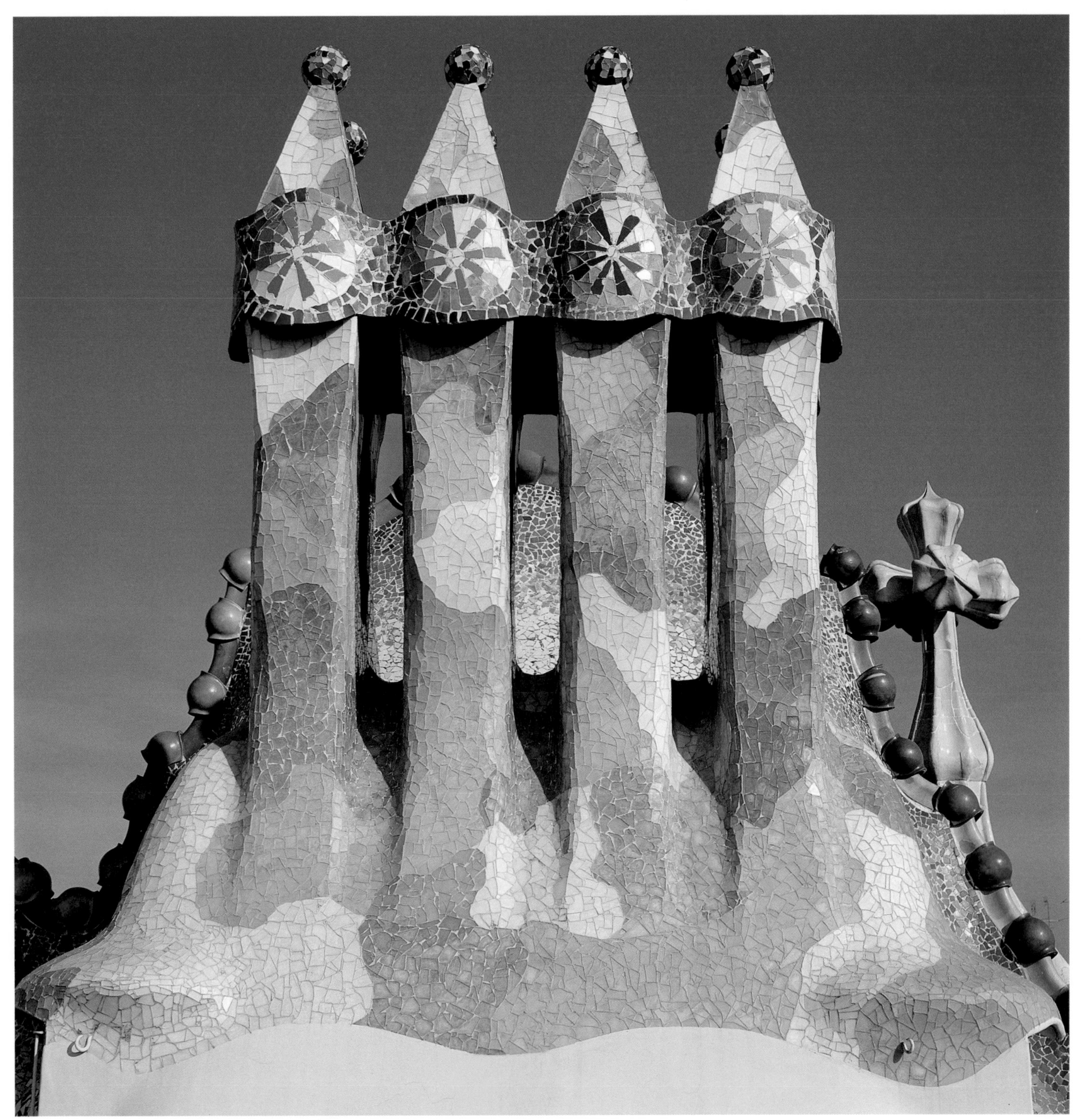

On the roof, by means of a sculptural treatment of the chimneys covered with ceramics and painted glass using the *trencadís* technique, Gaudí once again shows his passion for the dignifying of humble spaces, raising them to the category of work of art.

La Pedrera Casa Milà

Barcelona Passeig de Gràcia, 92

8

La Pedrera

1906-1912

Postcard from 1914.

Return to the origin

The La Pedrera was Gaudí's last piece of civil engineering work. It was built for Pere Milà and his wife, Roser Segimon. In this work, the architect abandoned the polychrome designs he had used on the Façade of the Casa Batlló, leaving the sinuous form of the stone to express itself with all its might.

The building, as futuristic as it is primitive, caused an extraordinary stir in the city. The many satirical cartoon strips that appear in the magazines of the time are an amusing example of the perplexity that La Pedrera must have caused amongst the Barcelona public.

The building is treated as though it were a giant sculpture. To build it, 1:10 scale plaster models were used that the sculptor Beltrán created following Gaudí's instructions. Once completed, the model was divided into parts and distributed amongst the stonemasons so that they would have the model for making the piece. When each piece was ready it was raised on a pulley set over the building's metallic structure. Once placed, the stonemasons hung down from the Façade on ropes so as to meticulously polish the joins and edges between the pieces of masonry. The result of this process was a gigantic building-cum-sculpture articulated around a metal skeleton that withstood the weight of the building and freed the load-bearing and other walls.

The La Pedrera is an exhibition of living architecture in which the undulation of the stone transforms weight into lightness, stiffness into movement and the inert into the organic.

Gaudí had a large group of collaborators who were able to develop his creative ideas, although the architect always supervised the final decisions. His commitment to the work was total, and the smaller details had exactly the same importance as the project as a whole. The architect's and his collaborators' tastes were not always well appreciated by the Milà family, a fact that led to relationships that could be described as turbulent to say the least. The most serious dispute broke out when Mr. Milà rejected the idea to crown the building with a sculptural set by Carles Mani. This piece of work, over four metres high, that should have been made in forged gold, represented the Virgin and Child flanked by the archangels Saint Gabriel and Saint Michael. The sculpture, according to the sketch by Joan Matamala, should have been placed over the m of the message sculpted on the Façade: AVE GRATIA M PLENA DOMINUS TECUM. Today, beneath the monogram of María, we can see a stone rose, a Marian allegory. Gaudí, for whom "the building was conceived as a homage to the Virgin", took the Milà family to court. The architect won the case and received compensation of 100,000 pesetas, a veritable fortune in those days, which he donated to charity. Roser Segimon had to wait until the death of the architect, in 1926, before daring to change the decoration of some columns.

The flat roof synthesises to perfection the treatment that throughout his architectural career, Gaudí devoted to the crowning elements.

The imposing undulating façade insinuates the life and movement of the stone.

BUS
TAX

La Pedrera

1906-1912

A huge residential building that was soon baptised by the Barcelona public as the La Pedrera, or stone quarry, due to its rocky outside appearance. Built in a mould-breaking architectural language, Gaudí did not finish the final stage of the project because of the differences he had with the owners.

The architect occupied a site of 1,620 m², over which he built on 1,323 m² as an undulating curve, both on the outside and the inside of the building, applying multiple solutions of controlled geometry as well as elements of a naturalist nature. In reality, the building is made up of two estates (with independent entrances but joined by the same Façade), and although each has a central courtyard, the owners' home covered the total surface area of the two.

Unlike the Casa Calvet and the Casa Batlló, the La Pedrera has a structure of stone, solid brick and metallic beams that release the Façade from the load-bearing functions and permit large openings for light and air to enter. This original feature, totally new compared to the traditional master walls, means that even today any partition can be knocked down without affecting the building's solidity, in an architectural precedent similar to that which some years later Le Corbusier would call "free plan". With the pillar system Gaudí was able to give different uses to the nine levels of the house. The basement was a garage for cars (the first underground car park in the city), the ground floor was for commercial establishments, the mezzanine for offices, the first floor the owners' home, the four upper floors for rent and the loft and attic for the laundry.

Over the latter part, configured by a series of walled up brick parabolic arches, Gaudí built the attic rooftop from which stand out amazing chimneys, ventilators and stairway exits of almost sculptural proportions. The rest of the building is also notable for the way in which it is resolved: the curious iron structure supporting the circular courtyard, the wide vestibules, the wrought iron balconies, the smooth plasterwork ceilings with dynamic relief work, the woodwork on the doors, windows and furniture, the design of the knobs, handles and peepholes, as well as a hydraulic flooring (originally designed for the Casa Batlló) of a hexagonal shape that Barcelona City Council took as a model to cover the pavements of Passeig de Gràcia.

In 1986 the La Pedrera, one of the symbols of Barcelona, was bought by the Caixa Catalunya financial entity, who, after restoring it, set up a space for temporary exhibitions and one permanent one: the Espai Gaudí.

National Heritage Site since 1969. UNESCO World Heritage Site.

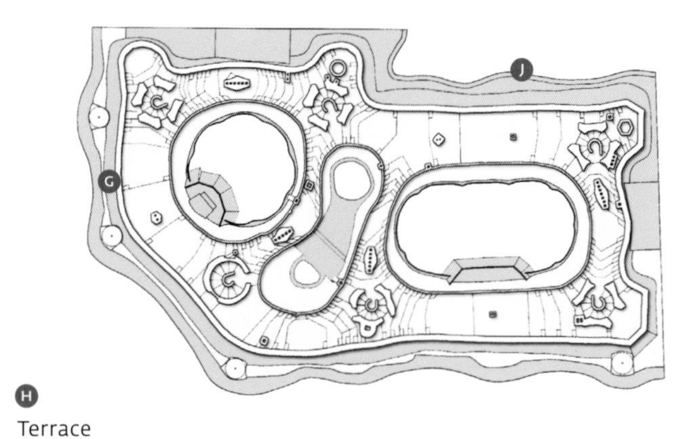

Terrace

Main floor

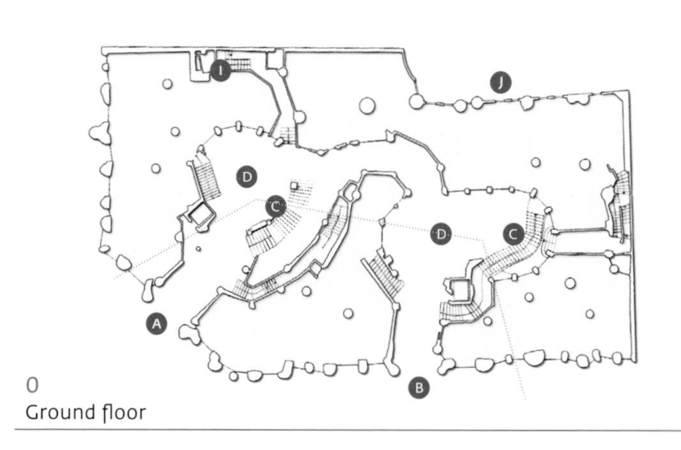

Ground floor

La Pedrera (Casa Milà)
Pere Milà i Camps, promoter
2nd of February 1906, project | 1906-1912, construction
Collaborators:
Josep Maria Jujol, Joan Rubió, Francesc de Paula Quintana, Domènec Sugrañes (architects)
Carles Mani (sculptor) Aleix Clapés, Iu Pascual (painters) Hermanos Badia (iron workers)
Casas Bardés (cabinetmaker) Joan Bertran (model maker) Mañach Workshops (foundries)
Josep Canaleta, Josep Bayó (contractors) Astilleros Morell (metallic structure)

A Entrance Passeig de Gràcia
B Entrance Carrer Provença
C Steps
D Vestibule
E Main floor
F Espai Gaudí loft
G Walkway
H Terrace
I Resident's stairway
J Rear façade

The railings of the balconies, authentic iron sculptures, were created by Jujol from the first one he designed and forged by Gaudí himself.

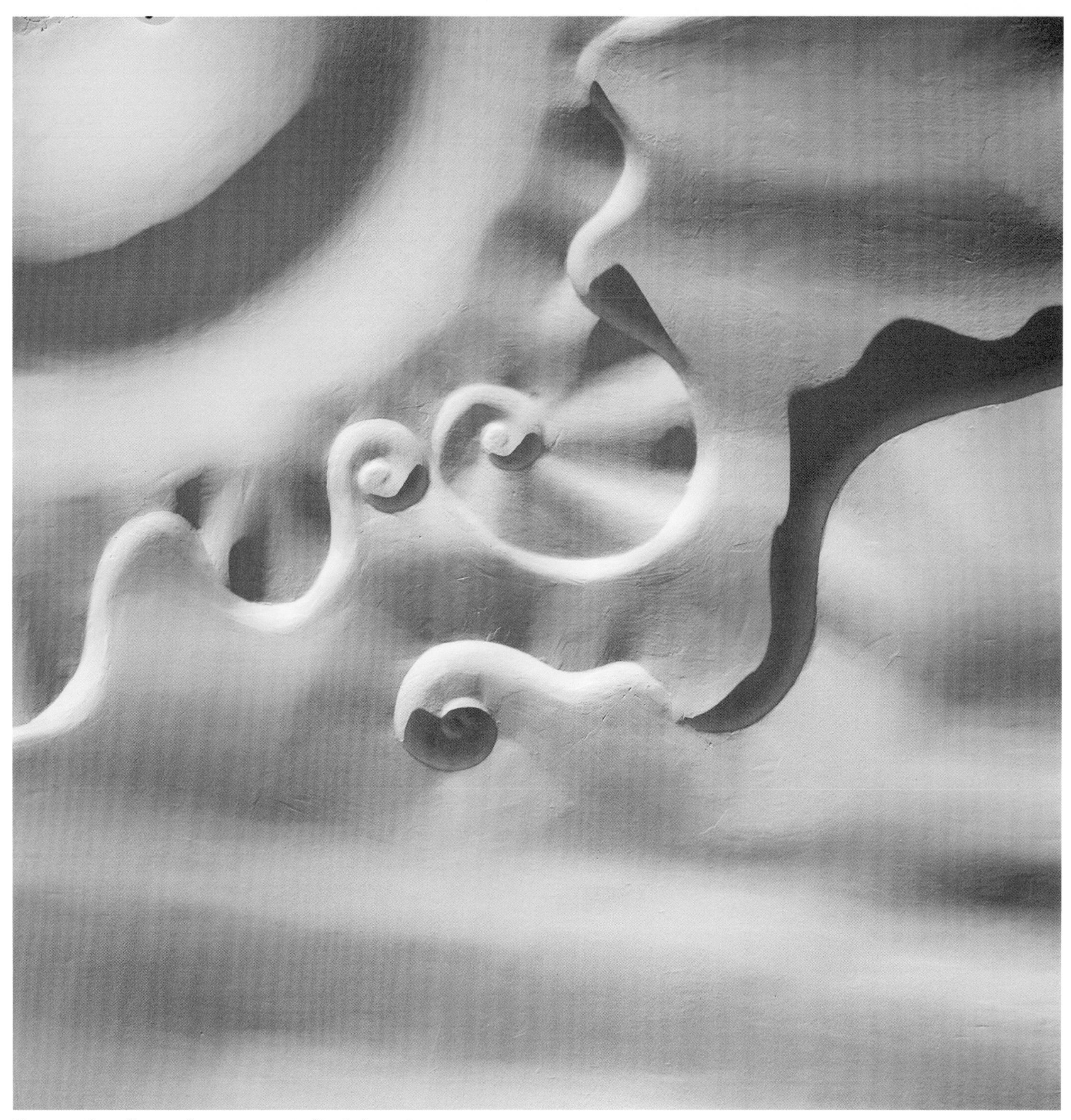

The sensation of harmonious movement of La Pedrera also appears in some ceilings that evoke the cadence of the seas.

The cast iron doors seem to imitate the cellular structure of an organism. Both the doors and the balconies of the façade are considered a precedent of abstract art.

The importance that Gaudí afforded the courtyards as distributors of light and ventilation reach their zenith in La Pedrera, where he turns them, both in terms of their size and architectural treatment, into veritable interior façades.

In the initial project, Gaudí weighed up the possibility of creating a spiral ramp that would climb the courtyard and enable cars to reach the landing of every floor.

Over the space of the inner courtyard, the flat roof of La Pedrera seems to soften and blend in with the walls of the loft. It is possible that Dalí, who even in 1933 reclaimed the figure of Gaidí passionately, found in him the inspiration for his soft forms.

Espai
Gaudí
La Pedrera
FUNDACIÓ CAIXA CATALUNYA

The loft is one of the most extraordinary spaces created by Gaudí. It is covered by a series of 270 partitioned catenary arches and different heights of an undulated and winding sequence that, as in Casa Batlló, was used as a washing and drying space.

The roof of the building recreates a dreamlike and suggestive world where the chimneys, ventilation ducts and stairway exits are transformed into attractive anthropomorphic forms about to begin some type of performance or ceremony.

The stairway exits that lead to the main façade are covered with *trencadís* of white marble and culminate in spiral forms crowned by crosses directed at the four cardinal points.

Perhaps the most popular figures of the flat roof of La Pedrera are the chimneys, plastered with lime mortar in ochre tones, which seem like silent guards that water erosion and the wind has sculpted in rock.

Crypt of the Colònia Güell

Cripta de la Colònia Güell

Santa Coloma de Cervelló **Colònia Güell**

9

Cripta de la Colònia Güell

1908-1915

A rehearsal for the temple

In 1890 Eusebi Güell founded an industrial village in Santa Coloma de Cervelló. The businessman's aim was to create a working atmosphere far removed from the workers' conflicts that were ravaging Barcelona.

The Còlonia Güell (Industrial Village) forms part of the ideological programme of the reformist movement advocated by León XIII in his encyclical Rerum Novarum. This was the first reflection made by the Church about the difficult situation of the working class in industrial society and in it is the proposal that the solution to the conflicts generated by urban industrialism is a worker-boss relationship based on catholic morality.

From 1898, the year in which Gaudí took charge of the project, until the first stone was laid, ten years went by. During this time Gaudí was working on a polyfunicular model, an ingenious system that consisted of hanging the ground plan of the building, drawn to scale, from the ceiling and hanging strings from it that formed the arches of the structure. From these arches were hung small sacks of pellets with a weight proportional to that of the loads they had to withstand. By this method, the architect obtained the shape of the vaulting with the inclination of the pillars and walls of the future building.

The structures used in the crypt were a rehearsal for the later work on the temple of the Sagrada Família. Gaudí began here to develop his particular metaphysical-constructive synthesis according to which, by means of the hyperbolic paraboloid he would build as "the angels build". As the architect himself said, "The wisdom of the angels consists in seeing questions of space directly without having to refer to the two-dimensional".

The complexity of the project meant that construction work moved at a slow pace and when Gaudí abandoned the work, in 1914, the only parts completed were the entrance portico, the crypt, the stairway that led to the church and the plinth of one of the bell towers. Nevertheless, the importance of its architectural solution has led it to be thought of as one of his fundamental pieces of work.

The industrial village, sold in 1943 by the heirs of Güell to the Bertrand i Serra family, stopped producing textiles in 1973. In 1984 it was sold to the Colònia Güell Consortium (University of Barcelona, Barcelona Regional Council and the Baix Llobregat County Council), the current conservationist of Gaudí legacy.

Photograph of the construction of the crypt around 1909.

Cripta de la Colònia Güell

1908-1915

A building devoted to worship for the workers of the Güell Industrial Village (Santa Coloma de Cervelló, Barcelona) from which it takes its name.

The portico is formed by a forest of leaning columns of basalt stone and brick that maintain an intimate dialogue with the surrounding landscape, made up mainly of pine trees. The columns support polygonal arches whose guidelines form a series of convex vaults of hyperbolic paraboloids that Gaudí decorated with ceramics in the shape of a cross. The crypt is reached by passing through the portico. It has a starred polygonal ground plan and pillars of brick, basalt or limestone, according to the loads they have to withstand.

The walls are covered with vitrified slag that came from the waste of the smelting furnaces, and the grilles of the large windows were made from recycled sewing machine needles. Everything, along with the *trencadís* mosaic, emphasises the idea of providing the humblest of materials with dignity.

Another remarkable aspect of the crypt is the abundant Christian iconography it contains: fish, the letters alpha and omega, which signify the beginning and the end, crosses, monograms of Christ, St. Andrew's crosses, etc.

For the interior, Gaudí designed the church pews and several stained-glass windows in suggestive chromatic shades, while Josep Maria Jujol was entrusted with the central altar. All these elements disappeared in 1936, when the crypt was ransacked and damaged, losing a part of the pews (reproduced in 1960), the stained-glass windows (restored in 1980) and the central altar (redesigned by Peter Harden in 1965). National Heritage Site since 1969. UNESCO World Heritage Site.

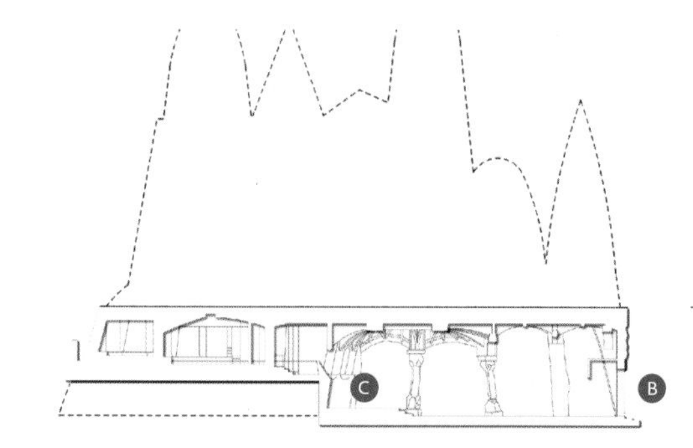

Church

Crypt

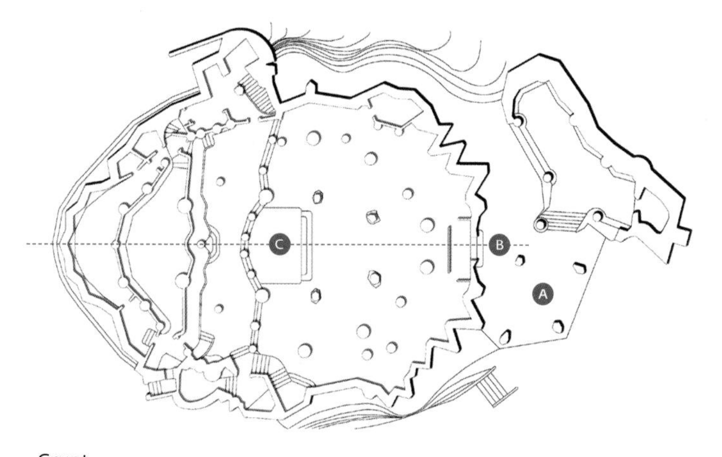

Crypt

Bench that combines wood and iron.

Model of the interior

Crypt of the Colònia Güell
Eusebi Güell i Bacigalupi, promoter
1898-1915, project | 1908-1915, construction
Collaborators:
Francesc Berenguer, Josep Maria Jujol, Josep Canaleta (architects) Eduard Goetz (engineer)

(A) Porch
(B) Entrance
(C) Altar

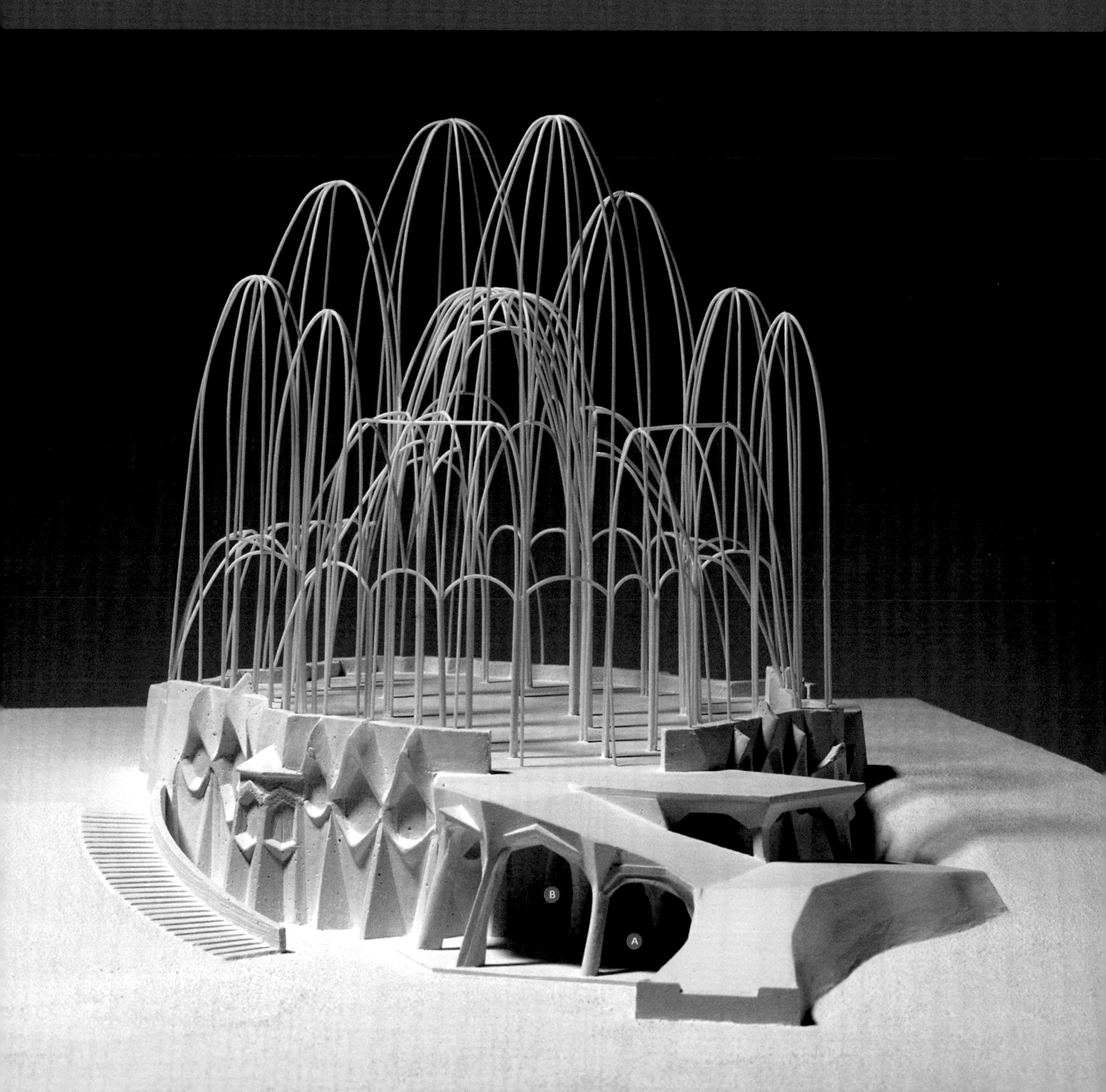

The crypt has large, irregularly-shaped windows. Nearly all of them have dust covers, bricks arranged irregularly and dark stones. All together it affords the whole piece a rustic appearance that integrates easily into the setting.

The crypt is characterised by the hyperboloid roof, the parabolic arches and the Catalan vaulting. The columns combine materials such as basalt, foundry slag, brick and ceramic and some are inclined to better withstand the load they bear.

The grilles that protect the stained-glass windows are made from loom needles from the Colònia Güell, a further example of Gaudian recycling. The needles are hooked together to form hexagons – a shape much-loved by Gaudí, a symbol of tenaciousness and community – with six-pointed stars in the centre.

The leaded stained glass windows illustrate large crosses, each one of a different design, based on flower petals (above), while the textures of the outside walls are achieved from stone, slag and brick.

Basílica de la Sagrada Família

Escoles de la Sagrada Família

Basílica de la Sagrada Família

Basílica de la Sagrada Família

Barcelona Plaça Gaudí

10

Basílica de la Sagrada Família

1883-1926
(currently under construction)

"My client is in no hurry"

In 1882 the Spiritual Association of Devotees of Saint Joseph, founded by Josep Maria Bocabella in 1866, began the construction of a temple in dedication to the Holy Family, or Sagrada Família. The temple, which should have been surrounded by gardens, had a solid purpose: "To awaken the drowsy hearts from their lack of enthusiasm, to exalt Faith, to give warmth to Charity, to make a contribution so that our Lord takes pity on the nation and that the nation, supported by its Catholic roots, thinks, preaches and practices the Virtues". In 1882, the architect Francesc de Paula del Villar began work on the crypt although a series of disagreements with the Board of Works about technical aspects of the project led to his resignation. In November 1883, Antoni Gaudí, then a young man of 31, took over the supervision of building work. He was recommended for the post by Joan Martorell although he didn't sign the first official document as architect of the Sagrada Família until 1884. Over the ground plan initiated by Villar, Gaudí erected the crypt maintaining the original neo-gothic style, although he improved some aspects in reference to the lighting. He surrounded the crypt with a pit that would allow natural light to enter while also protecting it from dampness. On the 19th of March 1885, the chapel of Saint Joseph was officially opened.

Original drawing by Gaudí of the finished temple.

In 1890 Gaudí drew up the first full plan of the Sagrada Família and this was possibly the year in which a large anonymous donation gave a boost to the temple's construction.Work on the Nativity Façade began in 1892. Two years later the neo-gothic apse was completed in which the spikes of the pinnacles and the amphibian and reptile gargoyles underlined the naturalist tendency of the decoration that the Nativity Façade would have.

For the great many figures on this Façade, Gaudí used a system of live moulding. He chose the model that best characterised the figure represented, placed them between mirrors and photographed them to obtain images from different viewpoints. After deciding on the most suitable posture, they were then moulded in plaster.

In 1910, in the hall of the Société Nationale des Beaux Arts de Paris, a model of the Nativity Façade was exhibited, polychromed by Jujol, along with a model of the bell tower culminating points. In the same year, Gaudí applied the new structural discoveries that he had rehearsed on the church of the Güell Industrial Village on the temple's naves. With these he overcame the limitations of Gothic, letting the weight of the building rest upon ramified and inclining columns, thus doing away with buttresses and enabling the opening up of large windows on the side walls. Gaudí took a special interest in the temple's acoustic conditions: the nave vaulting works as a diffusing element of both light and sound, and the openings of the bell towers are fitted with a *tornavoz*, a device for returning sound, leaning masonry plaques that protect from the rain and direct the sound of the bells towards the street.

Photograph of the crypt in construction published in 1886.

In 1911 Gaudí caught brucellosis and during his convalescence worked on the project for the Passion Façade. "I am prepared to sacrifice the building itself, to break vaulting and cut columns in order to get across the idea of how cruel sacrifice can be", he said. After the illness, the architect accepted no other commissions. In 1923 he found the definitive solution for the naves and roofing in 1:10 and 1:25 scale plaster models. The models that Gaudí left behind, partly destroyed during the Civil War, have enabled the works to be continued.

On the 30th of November 1925, the first bell tower of the Nativity Façade was completed, in dedication to Saint Barnabus. Gaudí stated his joy on seeing, "how that lance joined heaven and earth". On the 7th of June 1926, while on his way to the church of Sant Felip Neri, Antoni Gaudí was run over by a tram. He died three days after the accident and was buried in the crypt of the temple that he had devoted a great part of his life to. Gaudí's entire architectural career is encapsulated in the Sagrada Família, where he applied all the experience he had gained from his previous work. The initial neo-gothic style of the apse and the crypt, and the naturalism of the portals on the Nativity Façade evolved into the structural forms, based on controlled geometry and used in the temple's towers and naves. The sections show the different projects planned for the interior naves of the Sagrada Família. In the final solution of leaning, tree-like columns and vaulting that dispersed the light and sound, Gaudí achieved the synthesis of structure and form based on nature.

Current state of the works with the Nativity Façade in the centre.

Sanctus

Basílica de la Sagrada Família

1883-1926
(currently under construction)

The church, of basilican plan and with a Latin cross, has five naves in the central part and three in the transept. The limited area of ground where it had to be constructed (a single block in the Eixample district) meant that Gaudí took the fullest advantage of the space, which is why he placed the cloister around the temple.

The current state of the works, still in the process of construction, gives one an idea of the massive proportions the building will have once it is completed. It will have very high bell towers, the highest one, symbolising Jesus, will be 170 m tall. Around it will be built four more, which will represent the Evangelists. Another will be erected over the apse and will be in dedication to the Virgin Mary whereas to the eight existing bell towers (the Nativity and Passion Façades) will be added another four on the main Façade (in dedication to the Glory), which will symbolise the twelve apostles.

The style of the Sagrada Família is Gothic-based from developing controlled geometric structures. The work combines the essence of Gaudí's knowledge and constructive experience, featuring the paraboloidal base structure, the generation of the columns in the central nave and its tree-shaped form that supports vaulting of a hyperbolic base, as well as the interior modulation of the side windows that filter and distribute the light.

In the north-east corner, Gaudí set up his workshop, where he had the site office, a study space and the storeroom for archive material. It was here where he built the large-scale models, experimenting with the geometry, colours, forms and sounds; he designed the liturgical furniture of the temple, preserved his entire project and even stayed up all night working during the last months of his life. In 1936 the workshop was burnt down and the greater part of the project was lost, something that did not stop the work being continued and which is being carried on today.

Inscribed in the Architectural Heritage of Barcelona Catalogue. National Heritage Site since 1969. UNESCO World Heritage Site.

1 Nativity Façade
2 Glory Façade
3 Passion Façade
A Apse
B Central nave
C Altar
D Cloister
E Chapel of the Rosary
F Sacristy
G Baptistery
H Chapel of Penitence
I Schools

c/ Provença

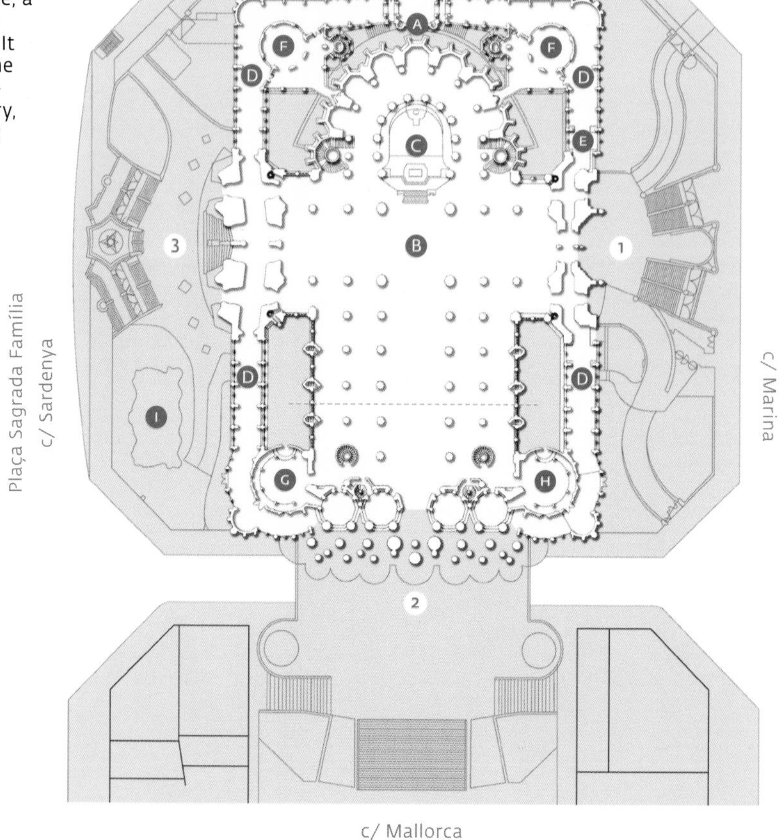

Nativity Façade around 1926.

Model of the central nave. >

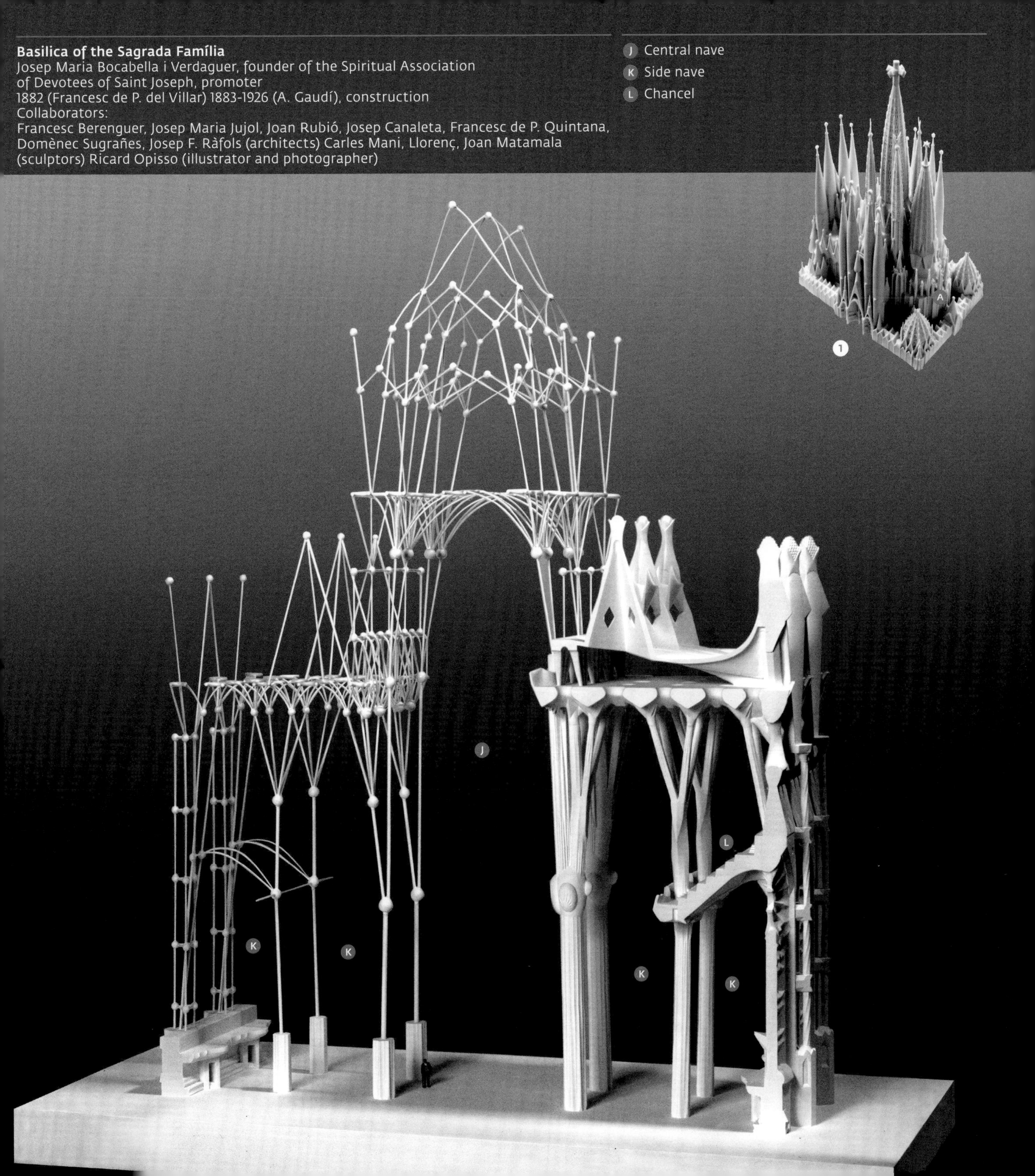

Basilica of the Sagrada Família
Josep Maria Bocabella i Verdaguer, founder of the Spiritual Association of Devotees of Saint Joseph, promoter
1882 (Francesc de P. del Villar) 1883-1926 (A. Gaudí), construction
Collaborators:
Francesc Berenguer, Josep Maria Jujol, Joan Rubió, Josep Canaleta, Francesc de P. Quintana, Domènec Sugrañes, Josep F. Ràfols (architects) Carles Mani, Llorenç, Joan Matamala (sculptors) Ricard Opisso (illustrator and photographer)

J Central nave
K Side nave
L Chancel

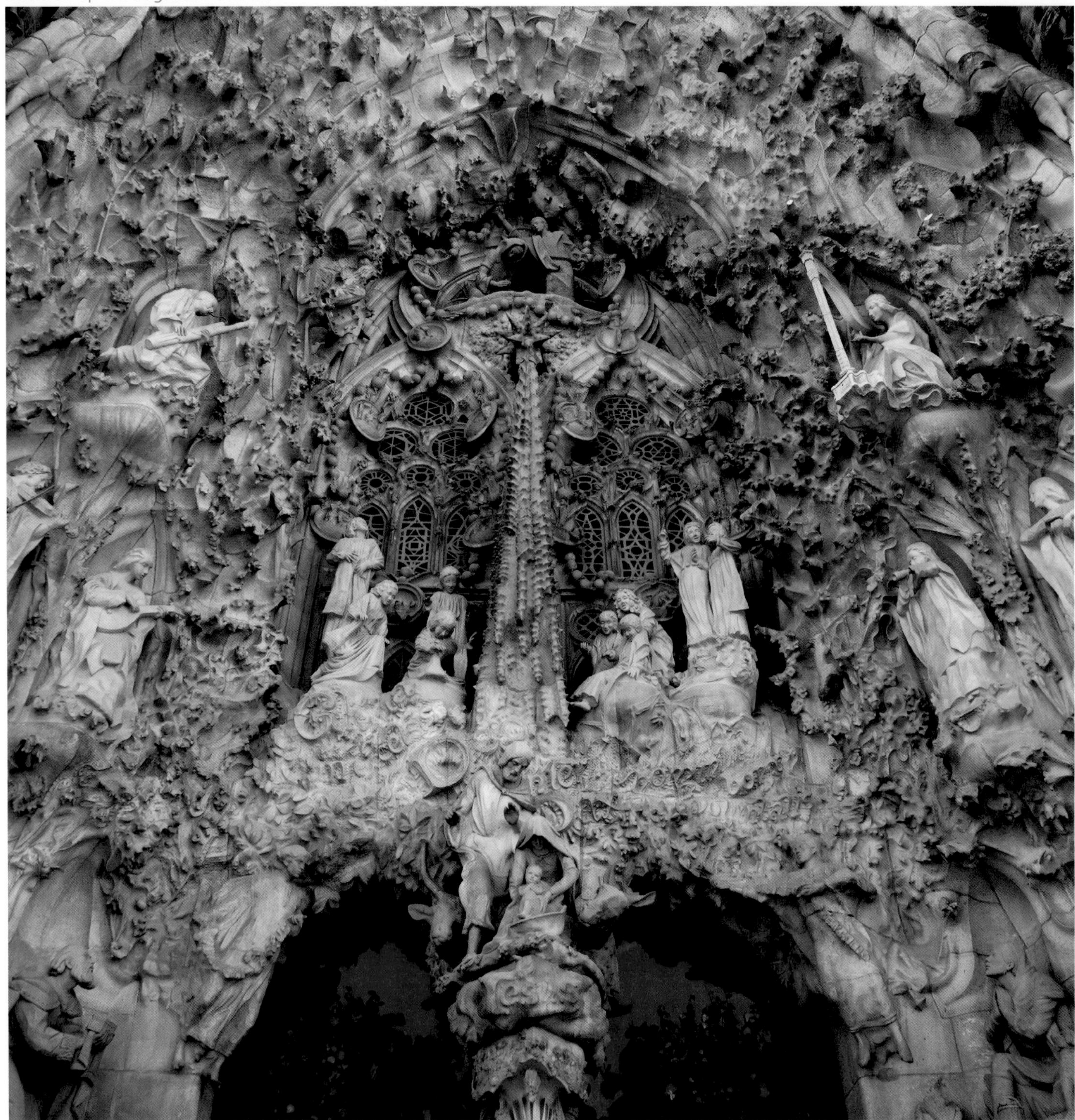

The Nativity Façade is presided over by the traditional figures of Bethlehem: Saint Joseph, the Virgin Mary, the Boy Jesus, the ox and the mule. Over them is raised the star that guided the Wise Men and they are surrounded by musician angels and cantors. This façade is an explosion of happiness, befitting the coming into the world of the Saviour.

Naturalist details of the Nativity Façade: the constellation of Gemini, different birds, aquatic flora and a chameleon about to catch an insect.

In the centre of the Nativity Façade, crowning the Charity Doorway, Gaudí placed a cypress tree, a symbol of resurrection and eternal life. It is crowned by the letter Tau with a cross and a dove (in allusion to the Holy Trinity). At the base of the cypress appears a pelican, an early Christian symbol of the Eucharist.

Gaudí placed the Crowning of the Virgin in a central spot of the Nativity Façade.

The Divine Providence – the hand that guides and the eye that sees all – crowning the Faith Doorway.

Pair of trumpeting angels announcing the Final Judgement. There are four angels, two above the column dedicated to Joseph and two above that of Mary.

Unlike the rejoicing that the Nativity Façade represents, regarding the Passion Façade, Gaudí stated in 1911: "I am prepared to sacrifice the construction itself, to break vaulting and cut columns to show how cruel sacrifice is". In 1987, the first sculptures by Josep Maria Subirachs began to be placed.

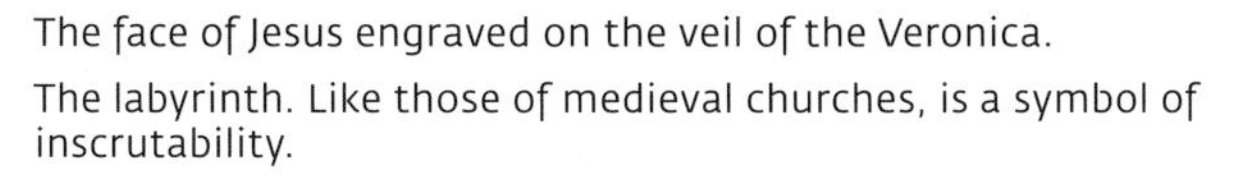

The face of Jesus engraved on the veil of the Veronica.

The labyrinth. Like those of medieval churches, is a symbol of inscrutability.

Detail of the crowning of the atrium of the Passion Façade.

The helmets of the soldiers are inspired by the crowning of the chimneys of the flat roof of La Pedrera.

View from the apse in its current state. In the centre, now visible is the tower dedicated to the Virgin, which will be crowned by a luminous star, the *Stella Matutina*. This tower, located above the crypt, at 140 m, will be the highest after that of Jesus.

Current state of the dome of the sacristy, which will be 40 m high. After the destruction of Gaudí's models during the Civil War, the reconstruction of the sacristy enabled the observation that the dome was formed with an intersection of 12 paraboloids joined in the upper vertex. This form is highly resistant and is what Gaudí also proposed for the central towers.

The nave reproduces the idea of the forest of columns which, like trees, branch out on reaching the vault.

The central nave seen from the apse. In the cross vaulting, the light of the Holy Spirit spills out and scatters all around the temple.

The dizzying turn of the stairs inside the towers takes us into the inside of a giant stone snail.

The towers of the three façades are dedicated to the twelve apostles, the first bishops of the Church. This is why they are crowned by pinnacles with the episcopal symbols: the mitre, staff, cross and ring.

Building work on the roof of the naves.

Infographic reconstruction of the appearance the temple will have once the works are completed.

Escoles de la Sagrada Família

Barcelona Plaça de la Sagrada Família

A dwarf at the feet of a giant

The Sagrada Família schools were built in 1909. This ephemeral building was erected on the spot where the main doorway of the temple should have been.

Elegant, innovative and simple, to Le Corbusier, one of the leading architects of the rationalist movement who visited Barcelona in 1928, this small building was more impressive than the temple itself.

The schools, built from a base of thin masonry walls, acquire structural robustness in both the walls and roofing thanks to its undulating form. The building's apparent simplicity bears witness to the expressive and structural strength of the use of controlled surfaces, in this case conoids.

The original building was destroyed in 1936, the year in which the Civil War broke out. Domènec Sugrañes rebuilt it, but it was once again destroyed in 1939. The person commissioned to undertake its second reconstruction was Francesc de Paula Quintana. The requirements of the current works have once again resulted in re-siting it.

Class inside the schools.

Gaudí built and financed from his own pocket the schools for the children of the workers of the Sagrada Família.

Ceiling of the schools where it meets the wall and in which one can see the undulation of the roof.

The building displays a wonderful movement on the most complex yet simplest roof ever seen.

Other works and projects

1876 Soffits in the Parc de la Ciutadella

After the deaths of his elder brother and mother when he was still an architecture student, to pay for his studies, Antoni Gaudí worked with two recognised professionals in Barcelona: Francesc de Paula del Villar and Josep Fontserè i Mestre.

The latter, author of the Mercat del Born, in 1873 won the competition for the urbanisation of the Parc de la Ciutadella and produced diverse constructions in it, such as the Monumental Waterfall.

For this Monumental Waterfall, among other elements, Gaudí produced two naturalist soffits placed on the rear part, one on each side of the entrance to the Aquarium, no longer there. Both soffits show a pair of salamanders between leaves of aquatic plants –different in each soffit– framed by an undulating ornamentation and with spirals.

1878-1879 Lampposts in Plaça Reial

The same year that Gaudí qualified as an architect, 1878, Barcelona City Council commissioned him with the production of models for monumental lampposts for the city. The report that Gaudí drew up was passed that summer, but they were not placed in Plaça Reial until September 1879.

These are two lampposts with six arms and a cast iron shaft and polished marble base. The column is crowned with a caduceus and winged helmet, both attributes of Mercury, the Roman god of commerce, and therefore a symbol of the commercial strength of Barcelona at that time.

The use of polychrome, so pleasing to Gaudí, who knew and admired the use that the ancients had made with colour, was favourably mentioned in publications of the time. Over the cast iron elements painted in grey, the reds and blues of the lampposts' arms and Mercury's caduceus and helmet stand out.

A year later four new lampposts were placed –of which only two remain– in the Pla de Palau. In this case they are a simpler model, with the same base and only three arms.

1879-1881 Mosaic of Sant Pacià

In 1850, the clerics of Jesús-Maria founded a college in Sant Andreu del Palomar, the current district of Sant Andreu in Barcelona.

The church of this college was built between 1876 and 1881 and the architect was Joan Torras i Guardiola, who built a large temple in neo-Gothic style, with a single nave with ribbed vaulting and high large windows, which on the austere exterior has a high bell tower.

A young Antoni Gaudí collaborated on the decoration of the interior of the nave. He produced the neo-Gothic altar, the monstrance in Byzantine style, the mosaic of the flooring and the lighting apparatus. During the Tragic Week, in 1909, the church suffered a fire of which only the mosaic was saved, which was fully restored between 1986 and 1989. It is a composition that covers the whole floor of the church, with predominantly geometric motifs and made with the traditional Roman technique called *opus tesselatum* (small pieces of between two and ten millimetres of stone, marble, etc., of different colours).

This mosaic by the young Gaudí is an antecedent of those he later produced in the dining room of Casa Vicens and in the crypt of the Sagrada Família.

1893 Project for the missions in Tangier

Around 1892, Gaudí received a commission for the Franciscan fathers to design the building of the Catholic Missions of Africa in Tangier. This project was backed by Claudio López, Marquis of Comillas, for whom Gaudí had produced El Capricho between 1878 and 1892.

Along with the marquis, the architect had travelled to Tangier in 1891 and Tetuán to see the land and observe first-hand the local and traditional architecture of North Africa.

Due to reasons still not completely clear, but which could be related to the war of Melilla of 1893, the project that Gaudí signed that same year was never realised.

However, all the experts coincide in their praise of the project, above all for the fretwork of the paraboloid towers-bell tower, the clearest precedent of the towers of the Sagrada Família built quite a few years later. Also of note is that between the series of towers, there is a central one with the other four around it, just as it appears in the dome of the Sagrada Família.

1900-1902 Stained glass in the chapel of Vallgorguina

In the district of Vallgorguina, for the chapel of one of the farmhouses there, specifically Can Pujades, Antoni Gaudí designed two stained-glass windows that were produced in the prestigious Amigó workshops in Barcelona.

The stained-glass window of the Archangel Michael, measuring 75 × 24.5 cm, was placed in a side window of the chapel. The second and more spectacular, called the "Rossetó", the rose window, was in the oculus of the façade and measures 90 cm in diameter.

The central motif of this stained-glass window is the Divine Providence, an eye placed in an open hand, the hand that guides and the eye that sees all. Three circles, which form a triangle alluding to the Holy Family, surround the symbol of the Divine Providence. In the circle on the upper vertex appears the anagram of Jesus, while on the two lower vertexes are represented the anagrams of Mary (left) and Joseph (right).

The Divine Providence would appear later on, to be exact in the temple of the Sagrada Família, in the Faith Doorway of the Nativity Façade.

These stained-glass windows have today been restored and are on show in the National Museum of Art of Catalonia, in Barcelona.

1902 Entrance to the Miralles Estate

Ermenegild Miralles was a printer, framer and manufacturer of papier mâché tiles with his own patent. Gaudí had used these floor tiles in the *fumoir* of Casa Vicens and that same year would use them in the decoration of the Cafè Torino.

Miralles, who owned an estate in Sarrià –very close to that of Eusebi Güell and in which Gaudí had produced the pavilions and famous Dragon gate–, commissioned the architect with the construction of the enclosure wall and the door of the entrance to the estate.

Remaining today of Gaudí's work are the door and short section of the wall. This has an undulating crowning and the body of the wall is also undulating vertically, which increases the sensation of dynamism and movement even more.

The door is double, with an entrance for carriages and another smaller one for pedestrians. The larger one has an unusual form of a lobulated arch and both are protected by a porch with small iron beams and fibre-cement material in the form of turtle shells. At the top of the door Gaudí placed a beautiful three-dimensional cross of cast iron, in undulating forms and of four arms.

1902 Cafè Torino

At the junction of Passeig de Gràcia and Gran Via, Flaminio Mezzalana, head of the Martini & Rossi vermouth in Spain, set up this establishment to publicise the drink in Barcelona.

For the decoration of the venue –which won the prize for the best establishment of the year awarded by Barcelona City Council– Mezzalana was able to count on the cream of the artists of the time: Ricard Capmany, Pere Falqués, Josep Puig i Cadafalch, Eusebi Arnau, Modest Urgell and, naturally, Antoni Gaudí.

The commission that Gaudí received –it is highly possible that Mezzalana was aware of the architect's early works, especially Casa Vicens– was the decoration of the Arab Salon of the Cafè Torino. Gaudí designed the wooden step and some pressed and varnished card tiles that were used to cover the walls and ceiling.

Unfortunately, the Cafè Torino, a magnificent example of the Modernist splendour of the Barcelona of the time, disappeared when in the early 1930s the building that housed it was demolished.

1904 Sala Mercè

In 1904, in La Rambla, very close to Plaça Catalunya, one of the first cinema theatres in Barcelona was opened. It was the Sala Mercè, a venue for shows of a singular nature, created by the painter Lluís Graner.

Gaudí designed the show hall with a decoration that imitated a cave, incandescence lanterns between coloured tulles and a floor that sloped down to the stage for better spectator visibility.

After the opening of the cinema theatre some grottoes were opened, with stalactites and stalagmites that imitated the caves of the Drac and which Gaudí discovered during his stay in Mallorca for the reform work on the Cathedral. These grottoes showed dioramas that changed periodically and which amazed the children and amused the grown-ups too.

In 1913, due to the economic difficulties that Graner was experiencing, the Sala Mercè finally closed.

1905 Catllaràs Chalet and Gardens of Can Artigas

Eusebi Güell, Gaudí's patron, founded the Portland cement company, Asland. He built the first factory in Catalonia in Castellar de n'Hug, where the River Llobregat springs, in the foothills of the Pyrenees, and it opened in 1904.

Gaudí visited the area the following year at the invitation of Güell, who had also bought the Catllaràs coal mine, very close to Castellar de n'Hug, in La Pobla de Lillet. Here he designed a chalet-refuge for the engineers of the mine.

The chalet still survives and is used as a refuge. It maintains its pointed shape and the attic-type windows similar to those he later designed for the attic of La Pedrera. Nevertheless, the adornments of the crowning and a very original double semi-circular stairway that led to the doors of the first and second floors have disappeared.

During his stay in La Pobla de Lillet, Gaudí was a guest in the home of Joan Artigas, who had a house alongside the rocky landscape of the source of the Llobregat. The architect designed some gardens integrated into the natural forms of the setting and to make them he had all the labourers who were working at that time on Park Güell to come expressly, where they carried out similar tasks on the viaducts.

Today the gardens are owned by the Council, have been restored, and can be visited.

1900-1916 I Mystery of the Glory (Montserrat)

At the end of the 19th century, it was decided to build a monumental rosary in Montserrat, the sacred mountain of Catalonia, on the path that leads to the Holy Cave, the place where, according to tradition, the image of the Virgin was found.

In 1900, the I Mystery of the Glory (the Resurrection of Christ) was entrusted to Antoni Gaudí, who, in the words of the then Abbot of Montserrat, Josep Deàs, "began by making a clearing of ground in order to have a cave, enlarging a smaller one that had been in the spot at the foot of the mountain and with the rocks and rubble forming a large square and raising some high walls in the form of towers".

The sculptures of the mystery were entrusted to Josep Llimona, who produced the image of Christ resuscitated in bronze and designed those of the angel, the sepulchre and the three Marias. However, a series of financial difficulties delayed them and they amended the project. The sculptures were finished by Dionís Renart and Jeroni Martorell was the architect in charge of completing the project, opened in 1916.

Gaudí situated the Christ in the place that on Easter Monday, more or less coinciding with the spring equinox, the image would receive the first ray of sun. Martorell changed the position, but it has currently been returned to its original position.

resurrexit
non est hic

1908 Hotel project in New York

Llorenç Matamala, sculptor, friend and collaborator of Gaudí, worked alongside the architect on the Sagrada Família, where he made several sculptures for the Nativity Façade. He also devoted time to collecting information about everything that happened in the world of Gaudí. This enabled him to know about the visit, in 1908, of two North Americans who would have proposed to Gaudí the construction of a hotel in New York and for which the architect would have designed some initial sketches.

This information did not appear in writing until 1956, the year in which Joan Matamala, also a sculptor and the son of Llorenç, wrote the report *Cuando el Nuevo Continente llamaba a Gaudí (1908-1911)* with five illustrations of drawings by Gaudí.

It was an organicist hotel standing some 360 metres in height in the form of a central tower surrounded by minor towers and a dome with immense interiors where five enormous dining rooms were superimposed, each one dedicated to the culinary culture of a continent.

Although the project never went beyond this, it would have been the tallest building in the world at the time, higher than the Eiffel Tower (the Empire State Building was not built until 1929-1931).

1910 Lampposts of Vic

For reasons of health, during the spring of 1910, Gaudí spent some weeks in Vic, where among other friends and acquaintances was the bishop of this diocese, Josep Torras i Bages.

In the autumn of the same year, Vic celebrated the centenary of the birth of an illustrious figure of the city: the philosopher and theologian Jaume Balmes. Gaudí was commissioned to come up with some ideas to embellish Vic.

Among other ideas, the architect suggested building two lampposts in the Plaça Major, the main square, facing the end of Carrer Verdaguer.

The lampposts were made under the supervision of Josep Canaleta, his assistant at the time in the Colònia Güell, and Josep Maria Jujol was entrusted to provide some gilded touches to the ironwork.

The lower part of the lampposts had a base and a shaft of large basalt stones and at the top projected the arms in cast iron from which hung panels shaped from the same material.

They were installed on the 7 September 1910 and demolished in 1924.

GAUDÍ
Singular architect

© Triangle Postals SL
Sant Lluís, Menorca
Tel. +34 971 150 451
triangle@triangle.cat
www.triangle.cat

Text:
© Josep Liz
Rossend Casanova, Antonio G. Funes

Photography:
© Pere Vivas, Ricard Pla
© Biel Puig, p. 9b, 173, 196
© Oleguer Farriol, p. 44
© Pau Giralt-Miracle, p. 51, 65, 81, 99, 127, 139, 201, 215
© Rafael Vargas, p. 120, 121
© Casa Batlló, p. 168, 170, 171, 172, 173, 174, 175, 176, 177
© Pere Vivas/Basílica de la Sagrada Família, p. 210, 224, 225, 226, 228, 230, 231
© Munch Museum/Munch Ellingsen Group/VEGAP, 2015, p. 14

Video:
© Hans Hansen, Biel Puig, Pere Vivas

Archive photographs:
Arxiu de la Càtedra Gaudí. ETSAB-UPC
Arxiu Històric de la Ciutat de Barcelona
Junta Constructora del Temple de la Sagrada Família
Museu Comarcal Salvador Vilaseca. Reus
Col·lecció privada Antoni González Moreno-Navarro
Col·lecció privada Juan-José Lahuerta

Editorial direction:
Ricard Pla

Computer graphics:
David Martínez

Plans:
CAIRAT, UPC, Joan Font

Translation:
Steve Cedar

Design:
Joan Colomer

Printed by:
CEGE
8-2015

Printed in Barcelona
Registration number: Me 399-2015
ISBN: 978-84-8478-661-0

TRIANGLE▼BOOKS

Acknowledgements:
Ajuntament de Mataró
Capítol de la Catedral de Mallorca
Casa Batlló
Casa-Museu Gaudí
Casa Vicens
Col·legi de les Teresianes
Consorci de la Colònia Güell
Fundació Catalunya-La Pedrera
Institut Municipal de Parcs i Jardins, Ajuntament de Barcelona
Junta Constructora del Temple Expiatori de la Sagrada Família
Museu d'Història de Barcelona
Obispado de Astorga
Palau Güell
Restaurant Casa Calvet
Restaurant Gaudí Garraf
Torre Bellesguard. Família Guilera
Daniel Giralt-Miracle
Carme Hosta
Juan-José Lahuerta
Anna Ribas
Beatriz Riu
Jaume Sanmartí
Silvia Vilarroya